T0108574

Cocoa Bombs™

Cocoa Bombs™

Over **40** make-at-home recipes for explosively
fun hot chocolate drinks

Eric Torres-Garcia

RYLAND PETERS & SMALL
LONDON • NEW YORK

Designer Geoff Borin
Editor Alice Sambrook
Head of Production Patricia Harrington
Art Director Leslie Harrington
Editorial Director Julia Charles
Publisher Cindy Richards

Chocolatier and Food Stylist Harriet Hudson
Drinks Stylist Lorna Brash
Prop Stylist Luis Peral
Indexer Vanessa Bird

First published in 2021
by Ryland Peters & Small
20–21 Jockey's Fields
London WC1R 4BW
and
341 E 116th St
New York NY 10029

www.rylandpeters.com

Text © Eric Torres-Garcia of Eric's Original Cocoa Bombs™
and Cocoa Bombs LLC (an Idaho Limited Liability Company)
2021

Design and photographs © Ryland Peters & Small 2021

ISBN: 978-1-78879-386-5

10 9 8 7 6 5 4 3 2 1

Printed and bound in China.

CIP data from the Library of Congress has been applied for.
A CIP record for this book is available from the British Library.

Notes

• Both American (imperial plus US cup) and British
(metric) measurements are included in these recipes;
however, it is important to work with one set of
measurements and not alternate between the two
within a recipe.

• Dark chocolate is defined as chocolate that contains
a minimum of 35% cacao (liquor or butter). Semisweet
chocolate, bittersweet chocolate and plain chocolate
are all terms used by manufacturers to label styles of
dark chocolate.

• When preparing cocoa bombs, especially to give as
gifts, take the following steps to maintain good kitchen
hygiene. Wash molds and equipment in hot soapy water
before use, keep work surfaces clear and clean, and wash
your hands frequently whilst working.

• Caution should be taken when handling any hot liquid,
from melted chocolate to milk. Always supervise young
children when serving them hot drinks.

MIX
Paper from
responsible sources
FSC
www.fsc.org   FSC® C008047

Contents

Introduction 6

Getting Started 8

CHAPTER 1 **The Classics** 26

CHAPTER 2 **Spice it Up** 42

CHAPTER 3 **Dessert** 58

CHAPTER 4 **Candy Corner** 74

CHAPTER 5 **Fun Time** 92

CHAPTER 6 **Seasonal Sensations** 106

Suppliers 124

Index 126

Acknowledgments 128

Introduction

What are cocoa bombs? Think of a bath bomb, but for milk. Now, before you run to the bathroom, you may want to continue reading on, because they work in a slightly different way. Cocoa bombs, in the simplest terms, are edible hollow chocolate spheres filled with fun little surprises. The very first bomb was made out of three essential ingredients: chocolate, marshmallows, and edible luster spray.

The recent craze for cocoa bombs can be traced back to a viral social media video of a prototype that was published by their creator, Eric Torres-Garcia, in December of 2019. Cocoa bombs have since gained legions of fans all over the world, with interested spectators rushing out to buy cocoa bombs, or hoping to find easy DIY methods to recreate this enticing, trendy treat at home.

In this recipe book, you will find step-by-step instructions, from the creator of the original cocoa bomb, on how to craft the perfect bombs—from making the shells to endless filling options, and how to smoothly seal the deal. You will need common kitchen items and little to no special equipment. There are hot cocoa classics, unique ideas for seasonal celebrations, and other whimsical concoctions.

Cocoa bombs are fast becoming a new holiday staple, and they make the perfect treat or gift at any time of year. We hope you enjoy this exciting way of drinking hot cocoa and trying out all the different flavors, there really is something for everyone.

Getting
Started

Equipment

To create the delicious recipes in this book, you will need most of the following kitchen tools.

Silicone molds
These will be used to make your cocoa bomb half-shells and should be roughly 2–2⅓ inches/5–6 cm in diameter. The half-sphere is the classic cocoa bomb shape, but in this book we have also used molds in the shape of hearts, eggs, and ducks—so the choice is yours! Silicone molds are widely available online in a variety of shapes.

Food-grade thermometer
Use this to check the temperature frequently as you temper your chocolate.

Microwave-safe glass bowl
For safely heating the chocolate.

Silicone spatula
For mixing the tempered chocolate.

Soup spoon
The back of a soup spoon is the perfect shape for smoothing melted chocolate inside the silicone molds. A normal spoon or pastry brush will also do the job.

Chocolate scraper or metal spatula/palette knife
For scraping the top of the mold.

Baking sheet lined with baking parchment
For demolding the chocolate shells.

Skillet/frying pan or microwave-safe ceramic dinner plate
This is heated and used for melting the rims of the half-shells slightly to stick them together.

Cupcake liners/cases
Useful to hold the bombs as you decorate.

Baking parchment, disposable sandwich bags, or pastry/piping bags
For piping the chocolate drizzle decoration.

Pastry or cake decorating brush
For painting on luster dust or melted chocolate decoration.

Ingredients

Cocoa bombs are usually made from three main ingredients: chocolate, hot cocoa mix/drinking chocolate powder, and marshmallows. The simplest version is a winning combo, but feel free to try new components and mix and match different recipes in this book to come up with your own creations.

Hot Cocoa Mix/Drinking Chocolate Powder

These are available in a wide variety of flavors. In this book we've made use of the classic milk, dark and white chocolate, as well as more exotic options like French vanilla, cookies and cream, and coconut. If you fancy something healthy, you can even use chocolate protein powder in its place.

Chocolate

As long as it's good quality, it doesn't matter whether chocolate bars or chips are used to make the shells. If you're using a bar, break it down into small pieces first—the smaller the pieces, the easier it is for the chocolate to melt evenly. Flavored chocolate, such as caramelized white chocolate or butterscotch chocolate, can also be used to good effect. Sugar-free chocolate or vegan chocolate both work well, if you prefer to use those.

Coffee and Tea

Different types of tea and coffee in powder form can be used to mix things up and complement the sweetness of the chocolate shell. Matcha green tea powder works exceptionally well with white chocolate, and frappe coffee powder is a great addition with all chocolate. Adding a shot of espresso to your finished hot cocoa drink takes the coffee element even further.

Spices

Warming spices like cinnamon, cayenne pepper, or nutmeg can be used to give a pleasing little kick to your cocoa bombs. Ready-made spice blends like chai or pumpkin spice are useful to have to hand.

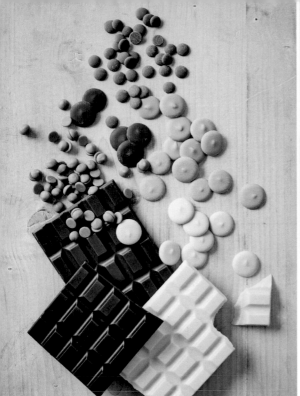

Extract Oils

These oils can be added to your tempered chocolate before it is set in the molds. Only a tiny amount is needed to give a big boost in flavor. They are available in a wide range of tempting flavors, such as raspberry, bourbon whiskey, orange zest, and hazelnut praline.

Marshmallows

Many of the recipes in this book use the widely available pink or white mini marshmallows, but feel free to get creative and use whatever other shape or color you like. Cinnamon twist, Christmas tree, or love heart-shaped are just some of the variations used in this book. Freshly made marshmallows would be a nice touch, if you plan on consuming the bombs within a few days.

Chocolate Spreads/Caramels

Other cocoa bomb fillings to make use of are sweet spreads like dulce de leche, Biscoff or hazelnut chocolate spread. These will make your hot drinks extra rich and decadent.

Crushed Candy

Your favorite candy can be crushed and added as a filling – we've tried peanut butter cups, fudge pieces, and peppermint candy.

Serving Suggestions

Milk, of course, is the classic base for cocoa bombs, whether dairy or plant-based. For a grown up version, a shot of bourbon whiskey, Irish cream, or other tipple of your choosing can be added.

Tempering Chocolate

There are two different ways to temper chocolate—in the microwave or in a double boiler. If you are on a short schedule and simply want to make a small, personal batch, opt for the microwave method. It will save you time, is more convenient, and it is easier to clean up. Each of the recipes in this book makes a small batch. If you are working with larger quantities, use the double boiler method and simply multiply the amounts according to the quantities you desire.

Microwave Method

Put two-thirds of the correct amount of chocolate for your chosen recipe in a microwave-safe glass bowl. Start heating it in the microwave for 35 seconds on high, then remove and stir. It will still be chunky, but stirring helps to distribute the heat evenly. Heat for another 30 seconds, then stir again. Repeat the process for 15 seconds, then 10 seconds thereafter, continuing until the chocolate is melted. Use your thermometer to make sure it reaches, but does not exceed, the melting temperatures specified on the opposite page. Once the chocolate has reached its melting temperature, add the remaining third of unmelted chocolate and stir until thoroughly combined. Allow to cool to the working temperature outlined on the opposite page and your chocolate will be tempered and ready to use.

Double Boiler Method

To temper your chocolate using the double boiler method, add 1–2 inches/2–5 cm of water to a saucepan and place it on the stove. Next, place a dry, shallow and heat-safe mixing bowl

over the top of the saucepan. The bowl should fit snugly on the saucepan rim to trap any steam underneath. Make sure the water in the pan does not touch the bottom of the bowl; to check, lift the bowl slightly and check if the base is dry before setting back down. Next, turn the stove to the lowest heat and add two-thirds of your chocolate to the bowl, according to the total amount specified in your chosen recipe. Use a food-grade thermometer to keep an eye on the temperature as the chocolate melts. Stir continuously with a heat-safe silicone spatula until all of the chocolate has melted and it has reached the correct melting temperature (see right). Turn the stove off and carefully remove the mixing bowl using an oven mitt. Add the remaining third of unmelted chocolate and stir until thoroughly combined and cooled to the specific working temperature (see right). The chocolate will now be tempered and ready to use. Letting your chocolate cool to its working temperature will give your bombs a shiny finish and help you avoid sugar/fat bloom and other issues.

Melting Temperatures

Whether you use the microwave or double boiler method, it is essential to let the chocolate reach the following temperatures before working with it. As a general rule of thumb, the lighter the chocolate, the lower the melting point.

Dark chocolate 114–118°F (46–48°C)

Milk chocolate 104–113°F (40–45°C)

White chocolate 104–109°F (40–43°C)

Working Temperatures

Once the chocolate you are using has reached its melting point, allow the chocolate to cool down to the following temperatures before working with it to avoid blooming and other issues.

Dark chocolate 82–88°F (28–31°C)

Milk chocolate 88–91°F (31–33°C)

White chocolate 80–84°F (27–29°C)

Making the Half-Shells

1 Before you start, make sure your chosen silicone mold has been rinsed well with hot water, is free of water spots and stains, and is completely dry.

2 Dip the back of a metal spoon (ideally a soup spoon or dessert spoon) into your tempered chocolate and begin evenly applying chocolate to the cavities from the bottom up. Run the back of the spoon from the bottom to the top edge of each cavity repeatedly to get a thick chocolate edge. Make sure the chocolate does not pool at the bottom of the cavities and try to distribute it as evenly as possible. If you are having trouble using a spoon, you can also paint the chocolate onto the cavities using a pastry brush.

3 After the cavities have been filled, clean off the excess chocolate by scraping the top of the mold using a small chocolate scraper. Scraping it will give your shells nice clean edges. If you don't have a chocolate scraper, you can use a clean ruler or a large metal spatula/palette knife. Scrape the chocolate back into the bowl if you want to use the leftover for decoration.

 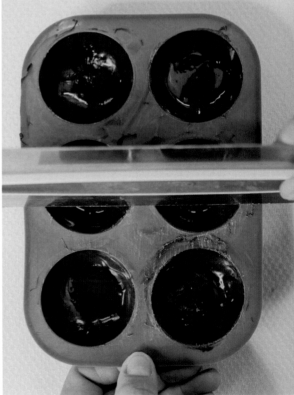

4 Place the mold in the fridge, facing downwards with something underneath to catch any potential drips, for about 3–5 minutes, or until the chocolate has set. Alternatively, you can leave the shells in the same position at room temperature for about 45 minutes, or until set. Repeat the coating, scraping, and setting process once or twice more, until your half-shells are as thick as you want them. Set any leftover tempered chocolate aside if you plan on using it for the drizzle decoration.

5 Once the chocolate has cooled and fully set for the final time, carefully place the silicone mold with the cavities facing down on a baking sheet lined with baking parchment. Begin demolding the shells one at a time by gently pushing from the back until the chocolate shell releases and pops onto the baking sheet. You are now ready to start filling (see next page).

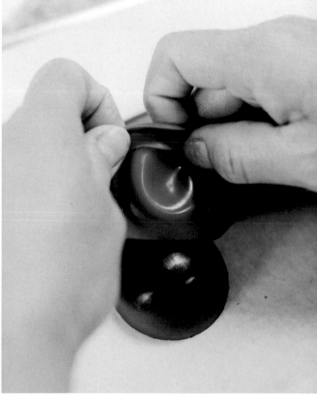

Filling and Sealing the Half-Shells

1 Now that all of the half-shells have been demolded, it is time to prepare to seal them together. Start by heating a non-stick skillet/frying pan over high heat for 30–40 seconds. Alternatively, you can also heat a microwave-safe dinner plate in the microwave for 30 seconds, or until just hot.

2 After you have slightly heated a pan or plate, make sure it is completely dry and place it near you on top of a heat-resistant pad or on a heatproof surface.

3 Balance a half-shell in the dip on a clean upside-down clean silicone mold (see below) or in a cupcake liner/case. Fill the shell first with the hot cocoa mix/drinking chocolate powder, then the marshmallows and/or other sweet treats, according to your chosen recipe. Be sure to avoid overfilling the shells to make the sealing process easier.

4 After you have filled the shell, grab another empty half-shell and place it rim-down onto the warm pan or plate. The rim of the

chocolate shell should slowly melt upon contact. Let the rim melt for 3–5 seconds only. Remove the shell from the heat and line up the melted rim with the dry chocolate shell containing your filling. Lightly press both halves together and hold for 8–10 seconds until set.

5 Wipe off any excess chocolate around the rim and voilà—you have successfully created your first cocoa bomb! Gently set it down on top of the upside-down silicone mold or in the cupcake liner/case and move on to the next one.

Decorating Techniques

Although there is already something beautiful about a simple, shiny chocolate sphere, there are many different ways to embellish your cocoa bombs further. From natural ingredients to candy toppings, drizzles, sprinkles, and more, the options are endless.

Sprinkles

An easy yet visually appealing decorative option, sprinkles come in countless different shapes and colors, from classics like vermicelli, stars, and nonpareil to spooky Halloween or Irish clover designs. Pick your niche theme and you will probably find a sprinkle that goes with it! It is best to apply sprinkles right after drizzling the bombs with melted chocolate to help them stay in place.

Cupcake Decorating Kits

Pre-made cupcake decorating kits, like the unicorn one used on page 101, are great for achieving a high-end, polished look. They can help you turn your cocoa bombs into gorgeous animals or characters.

Natural Ingredients

Natural ingredients are a great option for understated decoration, from coffee beans, orange peel, and crushed nuts to dried unsweetened shredded/desiccated coconut, freeze-dried berries, and homemade caramel. It is nice to reflect the flavors you have on the inside of the cocoa bomb by using them to adorn the outside.

Candy

In this book, marshmallows, caramels, candy eyes, mini fudge pieces, candy corn, chocolate drops, and crushed peppermints are just some of the confections that have been used to add decoration. Feel free to use your own favorite candy to add personal flair to your cocoa bombs. You may need to give heavier candy toppings a light push into melted chocolate drizzle to help them stick.

Cookies and Crackers

Whether you crumble them up to sprinkle over as a crumb or break them into smaller pieces to use as ears or arms, baked goods such as graham crackers/digestive biscuits, pretzels, and cookies are ideal for adding decoration to your bombs. They also bring a different texture and a hint of salt to balance the sweet.

Drizzles

For cocoa bombs that call for a chocolate drizzle decoration, you will need to temper an additional 2 oz./55 g of chocolate. You can do this in with the chocolate for the shells, or temper it separately when ready to decorate. (Leftover tempered chocolate may crystallize if left out too long, in this case simply reheat it using the same tempering method.)

Once the tempered chocolate is at working temperature, place it in a pastry/piping bag (or you can use a rolled up sheet of baking parchment or small sandwich bag with the tip cut off). Run a thin flow of drizzle across the top of the bombs in zig-zags, spirals, or patterns of your choice.

Candy melts are another option for creating drizzle toppings in bright colors. They do not need to be tempered, just melted before using.

Luster Dust

Use non-toxic edible luster dust to give a high-end, chic look to your bombs. These dusts come in various colors, but the gold and silver give a particularly stunning finish.

To give a light coating of luster, use a small pastry brush and dip only the tip of the brush into the dust—a little goes a long way. Gently tap the brush over the bomb so that the dust lightly falls onto the bomb in a natural pattern.

Alternatively, luster dust can be applied in specific places to add definition to characters, such as the rosy cheeks on the unicorn bomb (see page 101), or painted onto the silicone mold before the chocolate is added, to give a full coating or for a specific design.

Top Tips for Success

Here are some top tips to help you on your way, but remember, cocoa bombs require time and patience. Do not get discouraged if your first few attempts are not perfect—have some fun along the way!

● Always make sure you are working with chocolate that is accurately tempered to the specific temperatures given on page 15.

● Chocolate hates heat, so, if possible, try to work in a cool room.

● Never let dry or melted down chocolate (especially) come into contact with water.

● When applying the chocolate to the inside of the molds, make sure you use enough to avoid cracks or breakage during the demolding process. If you are unsure about whether your shells or edges will crack, an easy hack is to hold the silicone mold up to the light during the filling process and simply cover or brush over any transparent spots.

● Avoid overfilling your half-shells to make sealing them together easy. It is tempting to stuff in the filling, but your shells won't stick together properly or may break in half at a later point.

● When working with leftover tempered chocolate for the drizzle, if the chocolate has hardened a little and reached an in-between half-set state, just add a little gentle heat from a hair dryer to bring it to working temperature and it can be used again.

● Cocoa bombs should be stored at room temperature and not in the fridge or freezer. This is because chocolate is like a sponge; it absorbs moisture, as well as nearby aromas and/or flavors. To keep them at their best, store the cocoa bombs in a cool, dry place away from direct heat and sunlight.

Packaging and Serving Ideas

Cocoa bombs make perfect gifts or party centerpieces—they are unique, delicious, and can be personalised according to taste. They look impressive, but once you've mastered the technique they are easy to make. Whether you are gifting or celebrating with co-workers, your partner, children, or friends, you want to package or display your precious bombs in a way that appeals. Here are some ideas to try.

Gift Packaging Ideas

The key to packaging cocoa bombs as gifts is to line containers with plenty of tissue paper to prevent breakages. Not only does it keep the bombs safe, but you can also choose your paper in a complementing shade. You can also buy universal cardboard dividers online in varying sizes; place these inside packaging to hold the bombs separately in place and keep them from rolling around. Don't forget to add ribbons, stickers, gift tags, or even confetti to your parcel to make it extra-special. Some ideas for packaging are listed below:

• Cardboard cake boxes or re-purposed decorated shoe boxes.

• Cookie/biscuit or cake tins.

• Clear plastic bags or cellophane tied with colorful ribbons.

• Giant cones made with decorative cardboard.

• Inside a cup (that you are also gifting).

• Colorful paper bags.

Serving Ideas

Once you've put in the hard work of making your own cocoa bombs, why not enjoy serving them to friends and family at home or making a feature out of them. Here are some different ideas to try:

• Host a cocoa bomb party—serve the bombs on a platter and guests can pick from multiple flavors. You can all enjoy hot cocoa drinks and watching the bombs explode together.

• Take it one step further and host a DIY cocoa bomb-making party. Make the shells yourself and then provide these to guests along with a selection of fillings and decorations. You may have to help everyone with the sealing part!

• Top a celebration cake with cocoa bombs. They are beautiful things in their own right, and should just be removed and set aside when the cake is cut. The lucky birthday recipient can enjoy a hot cocoa drink with their cake or use the bombs another time.

• Add them to your Christmas cookie platter for something a little bit different that will get everyone talking.

CHAPTER **1**

The Classics

Dark Chocolate Cocoa Bomb

With its bold and rich taste, dark chocolate is the classic way to indulge in the hot chocolate bomb experience. I recommend using dark chocolate with 60–70% cocoa solids for a sophisticated balance of sweet, creamy, and intense. Dark chocolate tends to be runnier when melted due to the high cocoa content, so be sure to work with the specific temperatures supplied on page 15.

12 oz./340 g tempered dark chocolate (see pages 14–15)

TO FILL

3 tablespoons dark chocolate hot cocoa mix/drinking chocolate powder

15–21 mini marshmallows

TO DECORATE

dark chocolate vermicelli sprinkles

TO SERVE

hot milk of your choice (allow about 1 cup/ 235 ml per serving)

MAKES 3 COCOA BOMBS

1　Use 10 oz./285 g of the tempered chocolate to make 6 cocoa bomb half-shells, following the instructions on pages 16–17, and remove them from the molds. Reserve the remaining tempered chocolate for drizzling.

2　Prepare 3 small cupcake liners/cases on a parchment-lined baking sheet, or use a clean silicone mold turned upside down. This will hold the bombs in place as you assemble and decorate them.

3　Following the instructions on pages 18–19, warm up a pan or plate—you will use this for sticking the half-shells together.

4　To fill your cocoa bombs, spoon 1 tablespoon of dark chocolate hot cocoa mix/drinking chocolate powder into a half-shell, then add 5–7 mini marshmallows, depending on space. Take care not to overfill the shells, as this will make sealing them difficult.

5　Take another empty half-shell and place it carefully, rim-down onto the warm pan or plate. Let the chocolate rim melt for 3–5 seconds, then gently press together with the filled half-shell to seal, following the detailed instructions on pages 18–19. Wipe off any excess chocolate around the rim and set aside in the prepared cupcake liner/case or on the upside-down silicone mold.

6　Repeat with the remaining half-shells and filling to make 3 cocoa bombs.

7　To decorate, drizzle over the remaining tempered chocolate following the instructions on page 22, then sprinkle with some dark chocolate vermicelli sprinkles. Leave for 15–20 minutes at room temperature to allow the decoration to dry.

8　Package the bombs as gifts, or to serve, place a cocoa bomb inside a cup or mug, pour over the hot milk of your choice and watch the bomb explode. Stir to mix evenly and serve warm.

Milk Chocolate Cocoa Bomb

Milk chocolate is by far the most popular flavor of chocolate across the world. Use this recipe to make milk chocolate bombs and save yourself the trouble of guessing what your guests or gift recipients may enjoy. This simple but decadent recipe will bring a smile to anyone.

12 oz./340 g tempered milk chocolate (see pages 14–15)

TO FILL
3 tablespoons milk chocolate hot cocoa mix/drinking chocolate powder
15–21 mini marshmallows

TO DECORATE
milk chocolate vermicelli sprinkles

TO SERVE
hot milk of your choice (allow about 1 cup/ 235 ml per serving)

MAKES 3 COCOA BOMBS

1 Use 10 oz./285 g of the tempered chocolate to make 6 cocoa bomb half-shells, following the instructions on pages 16–17, and remove them from the molds. Reserve the remaining tempered chocolate for drizzling.

2 Prepare 3 small cupcake liners/cases on a parchment-lined baking sheet, or use a clean silicone mold turned upside down. This will hold the bombs in place as you assemble and decorate them.

3 Following the instructions on pages 18–19, warm up a pan or plate—you will use this for sticking the half-shells together.

4 To fill your cocoa bombs, spoon 1 tablespoon of milk chocolate hot cocoa mix/drinking chocolate powder into a half-shell, then add 5–7 mini marshmallows, depending on space. Take care not to overfill the shells, as this will make sealing them difficult.

5 Take another empty half-shell and place it carefully, rim-down onto the warm pan or plate. Let the chocolate rim melt for 3–5 seconds, then gently press together with the filled half-shell to seal, following the detailed instructions on pages 18–19. Wipe off any excess chocolate around the rim and set aside in the prepared cupcake liner/case or on the upside-down silicone mold.

6 Repeat with the remaining half-shells and filling to make 3 cocoa bombs.

7 To decorate, drizzle over the remaining tempered chocolate following the instructions on page 22, then sprinkle each one with some milk chocolate vermicelli sprinkles. Leave for 15–20 minutes at room temperature to allow the decoration to dry.

8 Package the bombs as gifts, or to serve, place a cocoa bomb inside a cup or mug, pour over the hot milk of your choice and watch the bomb explode. Stir to mix evenly and serve warm.

White Chocolate Cocoa Bomb

For a lusciously velvety, creamy flavor, white on white hot chocolate bombs are my go-to. For best results, use a white chocolate that contains cocoa butter in its primary list of ingredients. White chocolate tends to burn easily, so be sure to work with the accurate temperatures supplied on page 15.

12 oz./340 g tempered white chocolate (see pages 14–15)

TO FILL

3 tablespoons white chocolate hot cocoa mix/drinking chocolate powder

15–21 white mini marshmallows

TO DECORATE

white chocolate vermicelli sprinkles

TO SERVE

hot milk of your choice (allow about 1 cup/ 235 ml per serving)

MAKES 3 COCOA BOMBS

1 Use 10 oz./285 g of the tempered chocolate to make 6 cocoa bomb half-shells, following the instructions on pages 16–17, and remove them from the molds. Reserve the remaining tempered chocolate for drizzling.

2 Prepare 3 small cupcake liners/cases on a parchment-lined baking sheet, or use a clean silicone mold turned upside down. This will hold the bombs in place as you assemble and decorate them.

3 Following the instructions on pages 18–19, warm up a pan or plate—you will use this for sticking the half-shells together.

4 To fill your cocoa bombs, spoon 1 tablespoon of white chocolate hot cocoa mix/drinking chocolate powder into a half-shell, then add 5–7 mini marshmallows, depending on space. Take care not to overfill the shells, as this will make sealing them difficult.

5 Take another empty half-shell and place it carefully, rim-down onto the warm pan or plate. Let the chocolate rim melt for 3–5 seconds, then gently press together with the filled half-shell to seal, following the detailed instructions on pages 18–19. Wipe off any excess chocolate around the rim and set aside in the prepared cupcake liner/case or on the upside-down silicone mold.

6 Repeat with the remaining half-shells and filling to make 3 cocoa bombs.

7 To decorate, drizzle over the remaining tempered chocolate following the instructions on page 22, then sprinkle each one with some white chocolate vermicelli sprinkles. Leave for 15–20 minutes at room temperature to allow the decoration to dry.

8 Package the bombs as gifts, or to serve, place a cocoa bomb inside a cup or mug, pour over the hot milk of your choice and watch the bomb explode. Stir to mix evenly and serve warm.

The Everything Cocoa Bomb

Sometimes in life, you can have it all! The everything bomb is a decadent, rich dark chocolate shell with white and milk chocolate decoration. The result is a bomb with a beautiful marbled finish.

1 oz./30 g tempered white chocolate (see pages 14–15)

1 oz./30 g tempered milk chocolate (see pages 14–15)

8 oz./225 g tempered dark chocolate (see pages 14–15)

TO FILL
3 tablespoons dark chocolate hot cocoa mix/drinking chocolate powder

15–21 mini marshmallows

TO DECORATE
gold star sprinkles

TO SERVE
hot milk of your choice (allow about 1 cup/ 235 ml per serving)

MAKES 3 COCOA BOMBS

1 Drizzle the inside of 6 mold cavities with tempered white chocolate, then with tempered milk chocolate in the opposite direction. Leave to cool and set for 30 minutes at room temperature or for 3–5 minutes inside the refrigerator.

2 Proceed to make 6 dark chocolate cocoa bomb half-shells using the tempered dark chocolate on top of the white and milk chocolate pattern (reserving a little chocolate for sticking the decorations on later), following the instructions on pages 16–17, and remove them from the molds.

3 Prepare 3 small cupcake liners/cases on a parchment-lined baking sheet, or use a clean silicone mold turned upside down. This will hold the bombs in place as you assemble and decorate them.

4 Following the instructions on pages 18–19, warm up a pan or plate—you will use this for sticking the half-shells together.

5 To fill your cocoa bombs, spoon 1 tablespoon of dark chocolate hot cocoa mix/drinking chocolate powder into a half-shell, then add 5–7 mini marshmallows, depending on space. Take care not to overfill the shells, as this will make sealing them difficult.

6 Take another empty half-shell and place it carefully, rim-down onto the warm pan or plate. Let the chocolate rim melt for 3–5 seconds, then gently press together with the filled half-shell to seal, following the detailed instructions on pages 18–19. Wipe off any excess chocolate around the rim and set aside in the prepared cupcake liner/case or on the upside-down silicone mold.

7 Repeat with the remaining half-shells and filling to make 3 cocoa bombs.

8 To decorate, use the reserved tempered chocolate to stick some star sprinkles onto each cocoa bomb. Leave for 15–20 minutes at room temperature to allow the decoration to dry.

9 Package the bombs as gifts, or to serve, place a cocoa bomb inside a cup or mug, pour over the hot milk of your choice and watch the bomb explode. Stir to mix evenly and serve warm.

Vegan Cocoa Bomb

Those who follow a plant-based diet can enjoy a delightful cup of hot chocolate without missing out on the cocoa bomb party. These vegan bombs are made with vegan marshmallows and nature's sweetest gift to the world. Use almond, coconut, or other vegan milk of your choice to slowly pour over the bomb and watch the magic happen.

12 oz./340 g tempered vegan dark chocolate (see pages 14–15)

TO FILL

3 tablespoons pure cocoa powder

15–21 vegan white mini marshmallows

TO DECORATE

vegan white mini marshmallows

TO SERVE

hot vegan milk of your choice, such as almond or coconut (allow about 1 cup/235 ml per serving)

MAKES 3 COCOA BOMBS

1 Use 10 oz./285 g of the tempered chocolate to make 6 cocoa bomb half-shells, following the instructions on pages 16–17, and remove them from the molds. Reserve the remaining tempered chocolate for drizzling.

2 Prepare 3 small cupcake liners/cases on a parchment-lined baking sheet, or use a clean silicone mold turned upside down. This will hold the bombs in place as you assemble and decorate them.

3 Following the instructions on pages 18–19, warm up a pan or plate—you will use this for sticking the half-shells together.

4 To fill your cocoa bombs, spoon 1 tablespoon of pure cocoa powder into a half-shell, then add 5–7 vegan mini marshmallows, depending on space. Take care not to overfill the shells, as this will make sealing them difficult.

5 Take another empty half-shell and place it carefully, rim-down onto the warm pan or plate. Let the chocolate rim melt for 3–5 seconds, then gently press together with the filled half-shell to seal, following the detailed instructions on pages 18–19. Wipe off any excess chocolate around the rim and set aside in the prepared cupcake liner/case or on the upside-down silicone mold.

6 Repeat with the remaining half-shells and filling to make 3 cocoa bombs.

7 To decorate, drizzle over the remaining tempered vegan chocolate following the instructions on page 22, then top each one with some vegan white mini marshmallows. Leave for 15–20 minutes at room temperature to allow the decoration to dry.

8 Package the bombs as gifts, or to serve, place a cocoa bomb inside a cup or mug, pour over the hot milk of your choice and watch the bomb explode. Stir to mix evenly and serve warm.

High-Protein Cocoa Bomb

Feel the need for sweet but don't want to drop the ball? This keto diet-friendly cocoa bomb is a protein-rich sweet treat that can be enjoyed minus the high sugar and carb count.

12 oz./340 g tempered sugar-free dark chocolate (see pages 14–15)

TO FILL

3 tablespoons fudge brownie (or chocolate) protein powder

15–21 white mini sugar-free marshmallows

TO DECORATE

fudge brownie (or chocolate) protein powder, for dusting

TO SERVE

hot milk of your choice (allow about 1 cup/ 235 ml per serving)

MAKES 3 COCOA BOMBS

1 Use 10 oz./285 g of the tempered chocolate to make 6 cocoa bomb half-shells, following the instructions on pages 16–17, and remove them from the molds. Reserve the remaining tempered chocolate for drizzling.

2 Prepare 3 small cupcake liners/cases on a parchment-lined baking sheet, or use a clean silicone mold turned upside down. This will hold the bombs in place as you assemble and decorate them.

3 Following the instructions on pages 18–19, warm up a pan or plate—you will use this for sticking the half-shells together.

4 To fill your cocoa bombs, spoon 1 tablespoon of fudge brownie (or chocolate) protein powder into a half-shell, then add 5–7 mini sugar-free marshmallows, depending on space. Take care not to overfill the shells, as this will make sealing them difficult.

5 Take another empty half-shell and place it carefully, rim-down onto the warm pan or plate. Let the chocolate rim melt for 3–5 seconds, then gently press together with the filled half-shell to seal, following the detailed instructions on pages 18–19. Wipe off any excess chocolate around the rim and set aside in the prepared cupcake liner/case or on the upside-down silicone mold.

6 Repeat with the remaining half-shells and filling to make 3 cocoa bombs.

7 To decorate, drizzle over the remaining tempered sugar-free chocolate following the instructions on page 22, then sprinkle each one with some protein powder. Leave for 15–20 minutes at room temperature to allow the decoration to dry.

8 Package the bombs as gifts, or to serve, place a cocoa bomb inside a cup or mug, pour over the hot milk of your choice and watch the bomb explode. Stir to mix evenly and serve warm.

White Chocolate Coffee Cocoa Bombs

The bitter richness of coffee is the perfect foil for the bright sweetness of white chocolate. Here, those two flavors meet and mingle. To serve, pour one shot of espresso over the bomb, followed by warm milk of your choice—the end result is a velvety smooth cup of hot cocoa.

12 oz./340 g tempered white chocolate (see pages 14–15)

TO FILL

1½ tablespoons white mocha frappe powder mix

15–21 mini marshmallows

TO DECORATE

3 coffee beans

white mocha frappe powder mix, for dusting

TO SERVE

3 shots (3 fl. oz./90 ml) hot espresso coffee

hot milk of your choice (allow about ¾–1 cup/190 ml per serving)

MAKES 3 COCOA BOMBS

1 Use 10 oz./285 g of the tempered chocolate to make 6 cocoa bomb half-shells, following the instructions on pages 16–17, and remove them from the molds. Reserve the remaining tempered chocolate for drizzling.

2 Prepare 3 small cupcake liners/cases on a parchment-lined baking sheet, or use a clean silicone mold turned upside down. This will hold the bombs in place as you assemble and decorate them.

3 Following the instructions on pages 18–19, warm up a pan or plate—you will use this for sticking the half-shells together.

4 To fill your cocoa bombs, spoon ½ tablespoon of white mocha frappe powder mix into a half-shell, then add 5–7 mini marshmallows, depending on space. Take care not to overfill the shells, as this will make sealing them difficult.

5 Take another empty half-shell and place it carefully, rim-down onto the warm pan or plate. Let the chocolate rim melt for 3–5 seconds, then gently press together with the filled half-shell to seal, following the detailed instructions on pages 18–19. Wipe off any excess chocolate around the rim and set aside in the prepared cupcake liner/case or on the upside-down silicone mold.

6 Repeat with the remaining half-shells and filling to make 3 cocoa bombs.

7 To decorate, drizzle over the remaining tempered chocolate following the instructions on page 22. Top each bomb with a coffee bean and a light dusting of white mocha frappe powder mix. Leave for 15–20 minutes at room temperature to allow the decoration to dry.

8 Package the bombs as gifts, or to serve, place a cocoa bomb inside a cup or mug and pour over 1 shot (1 fl. oz./30 ml) of hot espresso coffee, followed by the hot milk of your choice. Watch the cocoa bomb explode. Stir to mix evenly and serve warm.

CHAPTER 2

Spice it Up

Spiced Chai Cocoa Bombs

One for the hot cocoa connoisseur who wants to spice up their chocolate bomb game. This comforting beverage will satisfy your chai latte and chocolate cravings all at once. Be warned though, it will leave you wanting more as soon as you are finished!

12 oz./340 g tempered dark chocolate (see pages 14–15)

TO FILL

3 tablespoons spiced chai tea latte powder mix

15–21 mini marshmallows

TO DECORATE

ground cinnamon, for dusting

3 star anise pods

TO SERVE

hot milk of your choice (allow about 1 cup/235 ml per serving)

MAKES 3 COCOA BOMBS

1 Use 10 oz./285 g of the tempered chocolate to make 6 cocoa bomb half-shells, following the instructions on pages 16–17, and remove them from the molds. Reserve the remaining tempered chocolate for drizzling.

2 Prepare 3 small cupcake liners/cases on a parchment-lined baking sheet, or use a clean silicone mold turned upside down. This will hold the bombs in place as you assemble and decorate them.

3 Following the instructions on pages 18–19, warm up a pan or plate—you will use this for sticking the half-shells together.

4 To fill your cocoa bombs, spoon 1 tablespoon of spiced chai tea latte powder mix into a half-shell, then add 5–7 mini marshmallows, depending on space. Take care not to overfill the shells, as this will make sealing them difficult.

5 Take another empty half-shell and place it carefully, rim-down onto the warm pan or plate. Let the chocolate rim melt for 3–5 seconds, then gently press together with the filled half-shell to seal, following the detailed instructions on pages 18–19. Wipe off any excess chocolate around the rim and set aside in the prepared cupcake liner/case or on the upside-down silicone mold.

6 Repeat with the remaining half-shells and filling to make 3 cocoa bombs.

7 To decorate, drizzle over the remaining tempered chocolate following the instructions on page 22. Dust each one with a pinch of ground cinnamon and top with a star anise pod. Leave for 15–20 minutes at room temperature to dry.

8 Package the bombs as gifts, or to serve, place a cocoa bomb inside a cup or mug, pour over the hot milk of your choice and watch the bomb explode. Stir to mix evenly and serve warm.

Horchata

Horchata is a famous Mexican sweet drink made from rice, cinnamon, and evaporated milk. It's traditionally served cold, but sometimes the rules are meant to be broken (or bombed). If you haven't had a chance to try it, this may be the most memorable way of doing so.

12 oz./340 g tempered white chocolate (see pages 14–15)

TO FILL

3 tablespoons horchata drink powder mix

3 pinches of ground cinnamon

3 pinches of ground nutmeg

6–9 cinnamon twist or mini white marshmallows

TO DECORATE

ground cinnamon, for dusting

TO SERVE

hot rice milk mixed with a little evaporated milk (allow about 1 cup/ 235 ml rice milk and 1 tablespoon evaporated milk per serving)

3 cinnamon sticks (optional)

MAKES 3 COCOA BOMBS

1 Use 10 oz./285 g of the tempered chocolate to make 6 cocoa bomb half-shells, following the instructions on pages 16–17, and remove them from the molds. Reserve the remaining tempered chocolate for drizzling.

2 Prepare 3 small cupcake liners/cases on a parchment-lined baking sheet, or use a clean silicone mold turned upside down. This will hold the bombs in place as you assemble and decorate them.

3 Following the instructions on pages 18–19, warm up a pan or plate—you will use this for sticking the half-shells together.

4 To fill your cocoa bombs, spoon 1 tablespoon of horchata drink powder mix into a half-shell, then add a pinch each of cinnamon and nutmeg. Add 2–3 cinnamon twist marshmallows, depending on space. Take care not to overfill the shells, as this will make sealing them difficult.

5 Take another empty half-shell and place it carefully, rim-down onto the warm pan or plate. Let the chocolate rim melt for 3–5 seconds, then gently press together with the filled half-shell to seal, following the detailed instructions on pages 18–19. Wipe off any excess chocolate around the rim and set aside in the prepared cupcake liner/case or on the upside-down silicone mold.

6 Repeat with the remaining half-shells and filling to make 3 cocoa bombs.

7 To decorate, drizzle over the remaining tempered chocolate following the instructions on page 22, then sprinkle each one with a little ground cinnamon. Leave for 15–20 minutes at room temperature to allow the decoration to dry.

8 Package the bombs as gifts, or to serve, place a cocoa bomb inside a cup or mug, pour over the hot rice milk sweetened with evaporated milk and watch the bomb explode. Stir to mix evenly, add a cinnamon stick if you like, and serve warm.

Mexican Cinnamon Cocoa Bombs

These fragrant, spiced cocoa bombs will elevate your hot chocolate experience to the next level. Pair with a classic Mexican 'concha' (a sweet bread roll), cookies, or other delightful pastries for a fun and quick breakfast.

12 oz./340 g tempered dark chocolate (see pages 14–15)

TO FILL

3 pinches of ground cinnamon

3 pinches of cayenne pepper

6–9 cinnamon twist marshmallows

TO DECORATE

coarse sugar crystals

ground cinnamon, for dusting

TO SERVE

hot milk of your choice (allow about 1 cup/ 235 ml per serving)

MAKES 3 COCOA BOMBS

1 Use 10 oz./285 g of the tempered chocolate to make 6 cocoa bomb half-shells, following the instructions on pages 16–17, and remove them from the molds. Reserve the remaining tempered chocolate for drizzling.

2 Prepare 3 small cupcake liners/cases on a parchment-lined baking sheet, or use a clean silicone mold turned upside down. This will hold the bombs in place as you assemble and decorate them.

3 Following the instructions on pages 18–19 warm up a pan or plate—you will use this for sticking the half-shells together.

4 To fill your cocoa bombs, add a pinch of ground cinnamon, a pinch of cayenne pepper and 2–3 cinnamon twist marshmallows to a half-shell, depending on space. Take care not to overfill the shells, as this will make sealing them difficult.

5 Take another empty half-shell and place it carefully, rim-down onto the warm pan or plate. Let the chocolate rim melt for 3–5 seconds, then gently press together with the filled half-shell to seal, following the detailed instructions on pages 18–19. Wipe off any excess chocolate around the rim and set aside in the prepared cupcake liner/case or on the upside-down silicone mold.

6 Repeat with the remaining half-shells and filling to make 3 cocoa bombs.

7 To decorate, drizzle over the remaining tempered chocolate following the instructions on page 22. Sprinkle each one with some coarse sugar crystals and a dusting of ground cinnamon. Leave for 15–20 minutes at room temperature to allow the decoration to dry.

8 Package the bombs as gifts, or to serve, place a cocoa bomb inside a cup or mug, pour over the hot milk of your choice and watch the bomb explode. Stir to mix evenly and serve warm.

Mocha Breve Cocoa Bombs

Popping one of these in a mug is a fun twist on your morning coffee ritual that is sure to leave you smiling. Or, share the love by packaging these bombs as gifts and giving to your yawning co-workers on a Monday morning.

12 oz./340 g tempered dark chocolate (see pages 14–15)

TO FILL

3 tablespoons mocha frappe powder mix

15–21 white mini marshmallows

TO DECORATE

cocoa powder, for dusting

TO SERVE

3 shots (3 fl. oz./90 ml) hot espresso coffee

hot half and half milk/ double cream mixed with the same amount of full-fat milk (allow about ¾–1 cup/190 ml per serving)

MAKES 3 COCOA BOMBS

1 Use 10 oz./285 g of the tempered chocolate to make 6 cocoa bomb half-shells, following the instructions on pages 16–17, and remove them from the molds. Reserve the remaining tempered chocolate for drizzling.

2 Prepare 3 small cupcake liners/cases on a parchment-lined baking sheet, or use a clean silicone mold turned upside down. This will hold the bombs in place as you assemble and decorate them.

3 Following the instructions on pages 18–19, warm up a pan or plate—you will use this for sticking the half-shells together.

4 To fill your cocoa bombs, spoon 1 tablespoon of mocha frappe powder mix into a half-shell, then add 5–7 mini marshmallows, depending on space. Take care not to overfill the shells, as this will make sealing them difficult.

5 Take another empty half-shell and place it carefully, rim-down onto the warm pan or plate. Let the chocolate rim melt for 3–5 seconds, then gently press together with the filled half-shell to seal, following the detailed instructions on pages 18–19. Wipe off any excess chocolate around the rim and set aside in the prepared cupcake liner/case or on the upside-down silicone mold.

6 Repeat with the remaining half-shells and filling to make 3 cocoa bombs.

7 To decorate, drizzle over the remaining tempered chocolate following the instructions on page 22, then sprinkle with a dusting of cocoa powder. Leave for 15–20 minutes at room temperature to allow the decoration to dry.

8 Package the bombs as gifts, or to serve, place a cocoa bomb inside a cup or mug and pour over 1 shot (1 fl. oz./30 ml) of hot espresso coffee, followed by the hot half and half milk/double cream and whole milk. Watch the cocoa bomb explode. Stir to mix evenly and serve warm.

French Vanilla Cocoa Bombs

In certain situations, being described as vanilla can be a compliment—or maybe only if you happen to be a sweet treat, because in that instance sometimes simple is better. Just one taste of these French vanilla cocoa bombs can prove this concept.

1/8 teaspoon French vanilla extract oil

12 oz./340 g tempered dark chocolate (see pages 14–15)

TO FILL

3 tablespoons French vanilla flavor hot cocoa mix/drinking chocolate powder

15–21 white mini marshmallows

TO DECORATE

white vanilla vermicelli sprinkles

TO SERVE

hot milk of your choice (allow about 1 cup/ 235 ml per serving)

MAKES 3 COCOA BOMBS

1 Add the French vanilla extract oil to the melted tempered chocolate and mix well.

2 Use 10 oz./285 g of the tempered chocolate to make 6 cocoa bomb half-shells, following the instructions on pages 16–17, and remove them from the molds. Reserve the remaining tempered chocolate for drizzling.

3 Prepare 3 small cupcake liners/cases on a parchment-lined baking sheet, or use a clean silicone mold turned upside down. This will hold the bombs in place as you assemble and decorate them.

4 Following the instructions on pages 18–19, warm up a pan or plate—you will use this for sticking the half-shells together.

5 To fill your cocoa bombs, spoon 1 tablespoon of French vanilla flavor hot cocoa mix/drinking chocolate powder into a half-shell, then add 5–7 mini marshmallows, depending on space. Take care not to overfill the shells, as this will make sealing them difficult.

6 Take another empty half-shell and place it carefully, rim-down onto the warm pan or plate. Let the chocolate rim melt for 3–5 seconds, then gently press together with the filled half-shell to seal, following the detailed instructions on pages 18–19. Wipe off any excess chocolate around the rim and set aside in the prepared cupcake liner/case or on the upside-down silicone mold.

7 Repeat with the remaining half-shells and filling to make 3 cocoa bombs.

8 To decorate, drizzle over the remaining tempered chocolate following the instructions on page 22. Sprinkle each one with some white vanilla vermicelli sprinkles. Leave for 15–20 minutes at room temperature to allow the decoration to dry.

9 Package the bombs as gifts, or to serve, place a cocoa bomb inside a cup or mug, pour over the hot milk of your choice and watch the bomb explode. Stir to mix evenly and serve warm.

Pumpkin Spice Cocoa Bombs

Let's face it, autumn just isn't the same without pumpkin spice. Everything about this flavor just makes winter's approach seem a lot more enchanting. It's the first sign that the holiday season has arrived.

⅛ teaspoon pumpkin spice extract oil

12 oz./340 g tempered dark chocolate (see pages 14–15)

TO FILL

3 tablespoons pumpkin spice flavor hot cocoa mix/drinking chocolate powder

6–9 pumpkin-shaped marshmallows

TO DECORATE

pumpkin- or leaf-shaped sprinkles

TO SERVE

hot milk of your choice (allow about 1 cup/ 235 ml per serving)

MAKES 3 COCOA BOMBS

1 Add the pumpkin spice extract oil to the melted tempered chocolate and mix well.

2 Use 10 oz./285 g of the tempered chocolate to make 6 cocoa bomb half-shells, following the instructions on pages 16–17, and remove them from the molds. Reserve the remaining tempered chocolate for drizzling.

3 Prepare 3 small cupcake liners/cases on a parchment-lined baking sheet, or use a clean silicone mold turned upside down. This will hold the bombs in place as you assemble and decorate them.

4 Following the instructions on pages 18–19, warm up a pan or plate—you will use this for sticking the half-shells together.

5 To fill your cocoa bombs, spoon 1 tablespoon of pumpkin spice flavor hot cocoa mix/drinking chocolate powder into a half-shell, then add 2–3 pumpkin-shaped marshmallows, depending on space. Take care not to overfill the shells, as this will make sealing them difficult.

6 Take another empty half-shell and place it carefully, rim-down onto the warm pan or plate. Let the chocolate rim melt for 3–5 seconds, then gently press together with the filled half-shell to seal, following the detailed instructions on pages 18–19. Wipe off any excess chocolate around the rim and set aside in the prepared cupcake liner/case or on the upside-down silicone mold.

7 Repeat with the remaining half-shells and filling to make 3 cocoa bombs.

8 To decorate, drizzle over the reserved tempered chocolate following the instructions on page 22. Sprinkle each one with some pumpkin- or leaf-shaped sprinkles. Leave for 15–20 minutes at room temperature to allow the decoration to dry.

9 Package the bombs as gifts, or to serve, place a cocoa bomb inside a cup or mug, pour over the hot milk of your choice and watch the bomb explode. Stir to mix evenly and serve warm.

Bourbon Whiskey Cocoa Bombs

These irresistible boozy cocoa bombs are just perfect for celebrating, whether you're gifting them on Christmas Eve, serving for New Year's Eve, or bringing them along to spice up winter bingo nights.

⅛ teaspoon bourbon whiskey extract oil

12 oz./340 g tempered dark chocolate (see pages 14–15)

TO FILL

3 tablespoons white chocolate hot cocoa mix/drinking chocolate powder

15–21 white mini marshmallows

TO DECORATE

gold, silver and bronze nonpareil and star sprinkles

TO SERVE

hot milk of your choice (allow about 1 cup/ 235 ml per serving)

3 shots (3 fl. oz./90 ml) bourbon whiskey

MAKES 3 COCOA BOMBS

1 Add the bourbon whiskey extract oil to the melted tempered chocolate and mix well.

2 Use 10 oz./285 g of the tempered chocolate to make 6 cocoa bomb half-shells, following the instructions on pages 16–17, and remove them from the molds. Reserve the remaining tempered chocolate for drizzling.

3 Prepare 3 small cupcake liners/cases on a parchment-lined baking sheet, or use a clean silicone mold turned upside down. This will hold the bombs in place as you assemble and decorate them.

4 Following the instructions on page 18–19, warm up a pan or plate—you will use this for sticking the half-shells together.

5 To fill your cocoa bombs, spoon 1 tablespoon of white chocolate hot cocoa mix/drinking chocolate powder into a half-shell, then add 5–7 mini marshmallows, depending on space. Take care not to overfill the shells, as this will make sealing them difficult.

6 Take another empty half-shell and place it carefully, rim-down onto the warm pan or plate. Let the chocolate rim melt for 3–5 seconds, then gently press together with the filled half-shell to seal, following the detailed instructions on pages 18–19. Wipe off any excess chocolate around the rim and set aside in the prepared cupcake liner/case or on the upside-down silicone mold.

7 Repeat with the remaining half-shells and filling to make 3 cocoa bombs.

8 To decorate, drizzle over the remaining tempered chocolate following the instructions on page 22, then sprinkle each one with gold, silver and bronze nonpareil and star sprinkles. Leave for 15–20 minutes at room temperature to dry.

9 Package the bombs as gifts, or to serve, place a cocoa bomb inside a cup or mug, pour over the hot milk of your choice and watch the bomb explode. Add 1 shot (1 fl. oz./30 ml) of bourbon whiskey to finish. Stir to mix evenly and serve warm.

CHAPTER **3**

Dessert

Crème Brûlée Cocoa Bombs

A white chocolate hot cocoa is a rare thing to find out in the wild; more unique still is this white chocolate hot cocoa with a delicious caramel topping. Now you can bring the essence of this fine dessert to your mug.

12 oz./340 g tempered white chocolate (see pages 14–15)

TO FILL

3 tablespoons white chocolate hot cocoa mix/drinking chocolate powder

15–21 mini marshmallows

TO DECORATE

non-stick cooking spray

¼ cup/50 g granulated/caster sugar

TO SERVE

hot milk of your choice (allow about 1 cup/235 ml per serving)

MAKES 3 COCOA BOMBS

1 Make the caramel decorations first. Line a baking sheet with foil and spray it with non-stick cooking spray. Place a small saucepan over medium heat and add the sugar. Immediately stir continuously until all the sugar has melted into a golden-brown liquid caramel. Remove from the heat and cool for 30–40 seconds.

2 Dip a fork into the caramel and drizzle patterns over the foil. Let the caramel decorations cool and set for 5 minutes.

3 Use 10 oz./285 g of the tempered chocolate to make 6 cocoa bomb half-shells, following the instructions on pages 16–17. Remove from the molds. Reserve the remaining chocolate for drizzling.

4 Prepare 3 small cupcake liners/cases on a parchment-lined baking sheet, or use a clean silicone mold turned upside down. This will hold the bombs in place as you assemble and decorate them.

5 Following the instructions on pages 18–19, warm up a pan or plate—you will use this for sticking the half-shells together.

6 To fill your cocoa bombs, add 1 tablespoon of white chocolate hot cocoa mix/drinking chocolate powder into a half-shell, followed by 5–7 mini marshmallows, depending on space. Do not overfill.

7 Take another empty half-shell and place it carefully, rim-down onto the warm pan or plate. Let the chocolate rim melt for 3–5 seconds, then gently press together with the filled half-shell to seal, following the detailed instructions on pages 18–19. Wipe off any excess chocolate around the rim and set aside in the prepared cupcake liner/case or on the upside-down silicone mold.

8 Repeat with the remaining half-shells and filling to make 3 cocoa bombs.

9 To decorate, drizzle over the remaining tempered chocolate following the instructions on page 22. Top with the caramel decorations. Leave for 15–20 minutes at room temperature to dry.

10 Package the bombs as gifts, or to serve, place a cocoa bomb inside a cup or mug, pour over the hot milk of your choice and watch the bomb explode. Stir to mix evenly and serve warm.

Cappuccino Tiramisu Cocoa Bombs

Food culture is always evolving, people are always looking to try new things at the same time as looking back for inspiration. Here, the classic Italian dessert has been given a modern cocoa bomb makeover.

¼ teaspoon cappuccino tiramisu extract oil

12 oz./340 g tempered dark chocolate (see pages 14–15)

12 oz./340 g tempered white chocolate (see pages 14–15)

TO FILL
6 teaspoons pure cocoa powder

30–42 mini marshmallows

TO DECORATE
pure cocoa powder, for dusting

TO SERVE
3 shots (3 fl. oz./90 ml) hot espresso coffee

hot milk of your choice (allow about 1 cup/ 235 ml per serving)

MAKES 6 COCOA BOMBS

1 Add half the cappuccino tiramisu extract oil to the tempered dark chocolate and half to the tempered white chocolate, and mix well.

2 Use 10 oz./285 g of each tempered chocolate to make 6 white cocoa bomb half-shells and 6 dark cocoa bomb half-shells, following the instructions on pages 16–17. Remove from the molds. Reserve the remaining chocolate for drizzling.

2 Prepare 6 small cupcake liners/cases on a parchment-lined baking sheet, or use a clean silicone mold turned upside down. This will hold the bombs in place as you assemble and decorate them.

3 Following the instructions on pages 18–19, warm up a pan or plate—you will use this for sticking the half-shells together.

4 To fill your cocoa bombs, spoon 1 teaspoon of pure cocoa powder into a dark chocolate half-shell, then add 5–7 mini marshmallows, depending on space. Take care not to overfill the shells, as this will make sealing them difficult.

5 Take an empty white half-shell and place it rim-down onto the warm pan or plate. Let the chocolate rim melt for 3–5 seconds, then gently press together with the filled dark chocolate half-shell to seal, following the detailed instructions on pages 18–19. Wipe off any excess chocolate around the rim and set aside in the prepared cupcake liner/case or on the upside-down mold.

6 Repeat with the remaining half-shells and filling to make 6 cocoa bombs.

7 To decorate, drizzle the remaining tempered white chocolate over the dark side of 3 cocoa bombs and the remaining tempered dark chocolate over the white side of 3 cocoa bombs following the instructions on page 22. Finish with a light dusting of cocoa powder. Leave for 15–20 minutes at room temperature to dry.

8 Package the bombs as gifts, or to serve, place a cocoa bomb inside a cup or mug and pour over 1 shot (1 fl. oz./30 ml) of hot espresso coffee, followed by the hot milk of your choice. Stir to mix evenly and serve warm.

Cookies and Cream Cocoa Bombs

Delight your inner child with this classic flavor—it tastes like eating cookies with milk, but better! You get the best of both worlds with the creamy hot milk and white chocolate offset by the darker, slightly salted, cookie crumble.

5 whole vanilla creme-filled chocolate sandwich cookies, plus extra if needed

12 oz./340 g tempered white chocolate (see pages 14–15)

TO FILL

3 tablespoons cookies and cream flavor hot cocoa mix/drinking chocolate powder

15–21 mini marshmallows

TO SERVE

hot milk of your choice (allow about 235 ml/ 1 cup per serving)

MAKES 3 COCOA BOMBS

1 Start by splitting the chocolate sandwich cookies apart and separating the cookie part from the creme center. Using a food processor, grind only the cookie part to a fine dust and set aside.

2 Add 3 tablespoons of ground cookie dust to 10 oz./285 g of the tempered white chocolate and mix well, then use to make 6 cocoa bomb half-shells, following the instructions on pages 16–17. Remove from the molds. Reserve the remaining chocolate for drizzling.

3 Prepare 3 small cupcake liners/cases on a parchment-lined baking sheet, or use a clean silicone mold turned upside down. This will hold the bombs in place as you assemble and decorate them.

4 Following the instructions on pages 18–19 , warm up a pan or plate—you will use this for sticking the half-shells together.

5 To fill your bombs, spoon 1 tablespoon of cookies and cream flavor hot cocoa mix/drinking chocolate powder and 1 teaspoon of cookie dust (if using) into a half-shell. Add 5–7 mini marshmallows.

6 Take another empty half-shell and place it carefully, rim-down onto the warm pan or plate. Let the chocolate rim melt for 3–5 seconds, then gently press together with the filled half-shell to seal, following the detailed instructions on pages 18–19. Wipe off any excess chocolate around the rim and set aside in the prepared cupcake liner/case or on the upside-down silicone mold.

7 Repeat with the remaining half-shells and filling to make 3 cocoa bombs.

8 To decorate, drizzle over the remaining tempered chocolate following the instructions on page 22, and sprinkle with a little of the ground cookie dust. Leave for 15–20 minutes to dry.

9 Package as gifts, or to serve, place a cocoa bomb inside a cup or mug and pour over the hot milk of your choice. Watch the cocoa bomb explode. Stir to mix evenly and serve warm.

White Chocolate and Matcha Cocoa Bombs

Matcha and white chocolate are a match made in heaven. Here, matcha powder is added to the tempered chocolate shells and placed inside the bomb along with marshmallows. The resulting, delicately green cocoa bomb is beautiful in appearance and flavor.

1 tablespoon matcha powder

12 oz./340 g tempered white chocolate (see pages 14–15)

TO FILL

3 tablespoons matcha powder

15–21 green or white mini marshmallows

TO DECORATE

matcha powder, for sprinkling

TO SERVE

hot milk of your choice (allow about 1 cup/ 235 ml per serving)

MAKES 3 COCOA BOMBS

1 Add the matcha powder to 10 oz./285 g of the tempered white chocolate and mix well, then use to make 6 cocoa bomb half-shells, following the instructions on pages 16–17. Remove from the molds. Reserve the remaining chocolate for drizzling.

2 Prepare 3 small cupcake liners/cases on a parchment-lined baking sheet, or use a clean silicone mold turned upside down. This will hold the bombs in place as you assemble and decorate them.

3 Following the instructions on pages 18–19, warm up a pan or plate—you will use this for sticking the half-shells together.

4 To fill your cocoa bombs, spoon 1 tablespoon of matcha powder into a half-shell, then add 5–7 green or white mini marshmallows, depending on space. Take care not to overfill the shells, as this will make sealing them difficult.

5 Take another empty half-shell and place it carefully, rim-down onto the warm pan or plate. Let the chocolate rim melt for 3–5 seconds, then gently press together with the filled half-shell to seal, following the detailed instructions on pages 18–19. Wipe off any excess chocolate around the rim and set aside in the prepared cupcake liner/case or on the upside-down silicone mold.

6 Repeat with the remaining half-shells and filling to make 3 cocoa bombs.

7 To decorate, drizzle over the remaining tempered chocolate following the instructions on page 22, then sprinkle each one with a light dusting of matcha powder. Leave for 15–20 minutes at room temperature to allow the decoration to dry.

8 Package the bombs as gifts, or to serve, place a cocoa bomb inside a cup or mug, pour over the hot milk of your choice and watch the bomb explode. Stir to mix evenly and serve warm.

Dulce de Leche Cocoa Bombs

Dulce de leche is the Latin American rich, sweet sauce that looks similar to caramel but is made with milk and sugar. These indulgent cocoa bombs are perfect for sharing with friends and family on cold winter evenings or during holiday festivities.

12 oz./340 g tempered white chocolate (see pages 14–15)

TO FILL

3 teaspoons white chocolate hot cocoa mix/drinking chocolate powder

3 teaspoons dulce de leche

15–21 mini marshmallows

TO DECORATE
gold nonpareil sprinkles

TO SERVE

3 tablespoons heavy/ double cream

3 tablespoons dulce de leche (or sweetened condensed milk)

hot milk of your choice (allow about 1 cup/ 235 ml per serving)

MAKES 3 COCOA BOMBS

1 Use 10 oz./285 g of the tempered chocolate to make 6 cocoa bomb half-shells, following the instructions on pages 16–17. Remove from the molds. Reserve the remaining chocolate for drizzling.

2 Prepare 3 small cupcake liners/cases on a parchment-lined baking sheet, or use a clean silicone mold turned upside down. This will hold the bombs in place as you assemble and decorate them.

3 Following the instructions on pages 18–19, warm up a pan or plate—you will use this for sticking the half-shells together.

4 To fill your cocoa bombs, spoon 1 teaspoon of white chocolate hot cocoa mix/drinking chocolate powder into a half-shell, then add 1 teaspoon of dulce de leche and 5–7 mini marshmallows, depending on space. Take care not to overfill the shells, as this will make sealing them difficult.

5 Take another empty half-shell and place it carefully, rim-down onto the warm pan or plate. Let the chocolate rim melt for 3–5 seconds, then gently press together with the filled half-shell to seal, following the detailed instructions on pages 18–19. Wipe off any excess chocolate around the rim and set aside in the prepared cupcake liner/case or on the upside-down silicone mold.

6 Repeat with the remaining half-shells and filling to make 3 cocoa bombs.

7 To decorate, drizzle over the remaining tempered chocolate following the instructions on page 22, then sprinkle each one with some gold nonpareil sprinkles. Leave for 15–20 minutes at room temperature to allow the decoration to dry.

8 Package the bombs as gifts, or to serve, mix together the cream, dulce de leche, and hot milk, then place a cocoa bomb inside a cup or mug, pour over the sweetened milk mixture and watch the bomb explode. Stir to mix evenly and serve warm.

Raspberry Cocoa Bombs

Dark chocolate and raspberry come together in harmony in these luscious cocoa bombs. This recipe is a year-round favorite, but their fruity flavor is especially enjoyable as winter comes to an end and spring is sneak-peeking around the corner.

⅛ teaspoon natural raspberry extract oil

10 oz./285 g tempered dark chocolate (see pages 14–15)

TO FILL

3 tablespoons raspberry flavor hot cocoa mix/drinking chocolate powder

3 teaspoons freeze-dried raspberry powder

15–21 mini heart marshmallows

TO DECORATE

2 oz./55 g tempered white chocolate (see pages 14–15)

freeze-dried raspberry powder, for sprinkling

pink heart-shaped sprinkles

TO SERVE

hot milk of your choice (allow about 1 cup/235 ml per serving)

MAKES 3 COCOA BOMBS

1 Add the natural raspberry extract oil to the melted tempered chocolate and mix well.

2 Use the tempered dark chocolate to make 6 cocoa bomb half-shells, following the instructions on pages 16–17, then remove from the molds.

3 Prepare 3 small cupcake liners/cases on a parchment-lined baking sheet, or use a clean silicone mold turned upside down. This will hold the bombs in place as you assemble and decorate them.

4 Following the instructions on pages 18–19, warm up a pan or plate—you will use this for sticking the half-shells together.

5 To fill your cocoa bombs, spoon 1 tablespoon of raspberry flavor hot cocoa mix/drinking chocolate powder into a half-shell, then add 5–7 mini marshmallows, depending on space. Take care not to overfill the shells, as this will make sealing them difficult.

6 Take another empty half-shell and place it carefully, rim-down onto the warm pan or plate. Let the chocolate rim melt for 3–5 seconds, then gently press together with the filled half-shell to seal, following the detailed instructions on pages 18–19. Wipe off any excess chocolate around the rim and set aside in the prepared cupcake liner/case or on the upside-down silicone mold.

7 Repeat with the remaining half-shells and filling to make 3 cocoa bombs.

8 To decorate, drizzle the tempered white chocolate over each cocoa bomb following the instructions on page 22, then sprinkle each one with some freeze-dried raspberry powder and pink heart-shaped sprinkles. Leave for 15–20 minutes at room temperature to dry.

9 Package the bombs as gifts, or to serve, place a cocoa bomb inside a cup or mug, pour over the hot milk of your choice and watch the bomb explode. Stir to mix evenly and serve warm.

Butterscotch Apple Crisp Cocoa Bombs

The taste of fall/autumn is abundant in these butterscotch apple crisp/crumble inspired cocoa bombs. With tart, warm apple cider and sweet butterscotch chocolate, they are comfort in a cup.

12 oz./340 g tempered butterscotch flavor chocolate (see pages 14–15)

TO FILL

9 soft caramel candies

3 pinches of ground cinnamon

15–21 mini marshmallows

TO DECORATE

crushed hard caramel candies and mini fudge cubes

3 cinnamon sticks (optional)

TO SERVE

hot apple cider of your choice (allow about 1 cup/235 ml per serving)

MAKES 3 COCOA BOMBS

1 Use 10 oz./285 g of the tempered chocolate to make 6 cocoa bomb half-shells, following the instructions on pages 16–17. Remove from the molds. Reserve the remaining chocolate for drizzling.

2 Prepare 3 small cupcake liners/cases on a parchment-lined baking sheet, or use a clean silicone mold turned upside down. This will hold the bombs in place as you assemble and decorate them.

3 Following the instructions on pages 18–19, warm up a pan or plate—you will use this for sticking the half-shells together.

4 To fill your cocoa bombs, add 3 soft caramel candies and a pinch of ground cinnamon to a half-shell. Finish with 5–7 mini marshmallows, depending on space. Take care not to overfill the shells, as this will make sealing them difficult.

5 Take another empty half-shell and place it carefully, rim-down onto the warm pan or plate. Let the chocolate rim melt for 3–5 seconds, then gently press together with the filled half-shell to seal, following the detailed instructions on pages 18–19. Wipe off any excess chocolate around the rim and set aside in the prepared cupcake liner/case or on the upside-down silicone mold.

6 Repeat with the remaining half-shells and filling to make 3 cocoa bombs.

7 To decorate, drizzle over the remaining tempered butterscotch chocolate following the instructions on page 22, then sprinkle each one with crushed hard caramel candies and mini fudge cubes. Leave for 15–20 minutes at room temperature to dry.

8 Package the bombs as gifts, or to serve, place a cocoa bomb inside a cup or mug, pour over the hot apple cider and watch the bomb explode. Enhance the flavor even further by using a cinnamon stick as a spoon. Stir to mix evenly and serve warm.

CHAPTER 4

Candy Corner

Peanut Butter Cup Cocoa Bombs

The tantalizing sweetness of milk chocolate paired with the savory saltiness of peanut butter is a combination proven to stand the test of time. The excellence of this iconic duo in a cocoa bomb is no exception.

12 oz./340 g tempered milk chocolate (see pages 14–15)

TO FILL

3 tablespoons milk chocolate hot cocoa mix/drinking chocolate powder

3 crushed peanut butter cups

12–18 mini marshmallows

TO DECORATE

crushed peanuts or peanut butter cups

TO SERVE

hot milk of your choice, (allow about 1 cup/ 235 ml per serving)

MAKES 3 COCOA BOMBS

1 Use 10 oz./285 g of the tempered chocolate to make 6 cocoa bomb half-shells, following the instructions on pages 16–17. Remove from the molds. Reserve the remaining chocolate for drizzling.

2 Prepare 3 small cupcake liners/cases on a parchment-lined baking sheet, or use a clean silicone mold turned upside down. This will hold the bombs in place as you assemble and decorate them.

3 Following the instructions on pages 18–19, warm up a pan or plate—you will use this for sticking the half-shells together.

4 To fill your cocoa bombs, spoon 1 tablespoon of milk chocolate hot cocoa mix/drinking chocolate powder into a half-shell, then add 1 crushed peanut butter cup and 4–6 mini marshmallows, depending on space. Take care not to overfill the shells, as this will make sealing them difficult.

5 Take another empty half-shell and place it carefully, rim-down onto the warm pan or plate. Let the chocolate rim melt for 3–5 seconds, then gently press together with the filled half-shell to seal, following the detailed instructions on pages 18–19. Wipe off any excess chocolate around the rim and set aside in the prepared cupcake liner/case or on the upside-down silicone mold.

6 Repeat with the remaining half-shells and filling to make 3 cocoa bombs.

7 To decorate, drizzle over the remaining tempered chocolate following the instructions on page 22, then sprinkle each one with some crushed peanuts or peanut butter cups. Leave for 15–20 minutes at room temperature to allow the decoration to dry.

8 Package the bombs as gifts, or to serve, place a cocoa bomb inside a cup or mug, pour over the hot milk of your choice and watch the bomb explode. Stir to mix evenly and serve warm.

S'mores Cocoa Bombs

Typically enjoyed during camping trips, s'mores are traditionally made with marshmallows toasted over the open fire and chocolate squished between two graham crackers. These cocoa bombs are topped with graham cracker crumbs and broiled/grilled marshmallows—delicious!

12 oz./340 g tempered milk chocolate (see pages 14–15)

TO FILL

3 tablespoons milk chocolate hot cocoa mix/drinking chocolate powder

15–21 mini marshmallows

TO DECORATE

9 mini marshmallows

crushed graham crackers/digestive biscuits, for sprinkling

TO SERVE

hot milk of your choice (allow about 1 cup/ 235 ml per serving)

MAKES 3 COCOA BOMBS

1 Use 10 oz./285 g of the tempered chocolate to make 6 cocoa bomb half-shells, following the instructions on pages 16–17. Remove from the molds. Reserve the remaining chocolate for drizzling.

2 Prepare 3 small cupcake liners/cases on a parchment-lined baking sheet, or use a clean silicone mold turned upside down. This will hold the bombs in place as you assemble and decorate them.

3 Following the instructions on pages 18–19, warm up a pan or plate—you will use this for sticking the half-shells together.

4 To fill your cocoa bombs, spoon 1 tablespoon of milk chocolate hot cocoa mix/drinking chocolate powder into a half-shell, then add 5–7 mini marshmallows, depending on space. Take care not to overfill the shells, as this will make sealing them difficult.

5 Take another empty half-shell and place it carefully, rim-down onto the warm pan or plate. Let the chocolate rim melt for 3–5 seconds, then gently press together with the filled half-shell to seal, following the detailed instructions on pages 18–19. Wipe off any excess chocolate around the rim and set aside in the prepared cupcake liner/case or on the upside-down silicone mold.

6 Repeat with the remaining half-shells and filling to make 3 cocoa bombs.

7 To toast the mini marshmallows for the decoration, preheat your broiler/grill on high. Place the marshmallows on a baking sheet lined with baking parchment and broil/grill until lightly toasted.

8 Drizzle over the remaining tempered milk chocolate following the instructions on page 22, then add the toasted marshmallows and a sprinkle of crushed graham crackers/digestive biscuits. Leave for 15–20 minutes at room temperature to allow the decoration to dry.

9 Package the bombs as gifts, or to serve, place a cocoa bomb inside a cup or mug, pour over the hot milk of your choice and watch the bomb explode. Stir to mix evenly and serve warm.

Coconut Paradise Cocoa Bomb

Take your taste buds on a trip somewhere tropical with these coconut-infused cocoa bombs. Try serving them with hot coconut milk poured over for the full flavor experience.

10 oz./285 g tempered dark chocolate (see pages 14–15)

TO FILL

3 tablespoons toasted coconut flavor hot cocoa mix/drinking chocolate powder

3 pinches of dried unsweetened shredded/desiccated coconut

9–12 toasted coconut flavor marshmallows

TO DECORATE

2 oz./55 g tempered milk chocolate (see pages 14–15), for drizzling

dried unsweetened shredded/desiccated coconut

TO SERVE

hot coconut milk or milk of your choice (allow about 1 cup/235 ml per serving)

MAKES 3 COCOA BOMBS

1 Use the tempered dark chocolate to make 6 cocoa bomb half-shells, following the instructions on pages 16–17, then remove from the molds.

2 Prepare 3 small cupcake liners/cases on a parchment-lined baking sheet, or use a clean silicone mold turned upside down. This will hold the bombs in place as you assemble and decorate them.

3 Following the instructions on pages 18–19, warm up a pan or plate—you will use this for sticking the half-shells together.

4 To fill your cocoa bombs, spoon 1 tablespoon of toasted coconut flavor hot cocoa mix/drinking chocolate powder into a half-shell, then add a pinch of dried unsweetened shredded/desiccated coconut and 3–4 toasted coconut flavor marshmallows, depending on space. Take care not to overfill the shells, as this will make sealing them difficult.

5 Take another empty half-shell and place it carefully, rim-down onto the warm pan or plate. Let the chocolate rim melt for 3–5 seconds, then gently press together with the filled half-shell to seal, following the detailed instructions on pages 18–19. Wipe off any excess chocolate around the rim and set aside in the prepared cupcake liner/case or on the upside-down silicone mold.

6 Repeat with the remaining half-shells and filling to make 3 cocoa bombs.

7 To decorate, drizzle the tempered milk chocolate over each cocoa bomb following the instructions on page 22, then sprinkle each one with some dried unsweetened shredded/desiccated coconut. Leave for 15–20 minutes at room temperature to allow the decoration to dry.

8 Package the bombs as gifts, or to serve, place a cocoa bomb inside a cup or mug, pour over the hot coconut milk or milk of your choice and watch the bomb explode. Stir to mix evenly and serve warm.

Hazelnut Praline Cocoa Bombs

The nutty flavor and silky-smooth chocolate spread in this recipe create a sumptuous hot cocoa drink. It's the crowd-pleasing element to these cocoa bombs that makes them an excellent gift.

⅛ teaspoon hazelnut praline extract oil

10 oz./285 g tempered dark chocolate (see pages 14–15)

TO FILL
3 tablespoons hazelnut chocolate spread

15–21 mini marshmallows

TO DECORATE
2 oz./55 g tempered milk chocolate (see pages 14–15), for drizzling

crushed hazelnuts, for sprinkling

TO SERVE
hot milk of your choice (allow about 1 cup/ 235 ml per serving)

MAKES 3 COCOA BOMBS

1 Add the hazelnut praline extract oil to the melted tempered chocolate and mix well.

2 Use the tempered dark chocolate to make 6 cocoa bomb half-shells, following the instructions on pages 16–17, then remove from the molds.

3 Prepare 3 small cupcake liners/cases on a parchment-lined baking sheet, or use a clean silicone mold turned upside down. This will hold the bombs in place as you assemble and decorate them.

4 Following the instructions on pages 18–19, warm up a pan or plate—you will use this for sticking the half-shells together.

5 To fill your cocoa bombs, spoon 1 tablespoon of hazelnut chocolate spread into a half-shell, then add 5–7 mini marshmallows, depending on space. Take care not to overfill the shells, as this will make sealing them difficult.

6 Take another empty half-shell and place it carefully, rim-down onto the warm pan or plate. Let the chocolate rim melt for 3–5 seconds, then gently press together with the filled half-shell to seal, following the detailed instructions on pages 18–19. Wipe off any excess chocolate around the rim and set aside in the prepared cupcake liner/case or on the upside-down silicone mold.

7 Repeat with the remaining half-shells and filling to make 3 cocoa bombs.

8 To decorate, drizzle the tempered milk chocolate over each cocoa bomb following the instructions on page 22, then sprinkle each one with some crushed hazelnuts. Leave for 15–20 minutes at room temperature to allow the decoration to dry.

9 Package the bombs as gifts, or to serve, place a cocoa bomb inside a cup or mug, pour over the hot milk of your choice and watch the bomb explode. Stir to mix evenly and serve warm.

Salted Caramel Cocoa Bombs

This creation is filled with sweet caramel candy pieces, mini white marshmallows, caramel hot cocoa mix/drinking chocolate powder, and topped with a pinch of coarse sea salt flakes for double the taste sensation and just the right amount of subtle salty notes.

12 oz./340 g tempered dark chocolate (see pages 14–15)

TO FILL

3 tablespoons caramel flavor hot cocoa mix/drinking chocolate powder

9 caramel candy pieces

15–21 white mini marshmallows

TO DECORATE

caramel candy pieces

coarse sea salt, for sprinkling

TO SERVE

hot milk of your choice (allow about 1 cup/235 ml per serving)

MAKES 3 COCOA BOMBS

1 Use 10 oz./285 g of the tempered chocolate to make 6 cocoa bomb half-shells, following the instructions on pages 16–17. Remove from the molds. Reserve the remaining chocolate for drizzling.

2 Prepare 3 small cupcake liners/cases on a parchment-lined baking sheet, or use a clean silicone mold turned upside down. This will hold the bombs in place as you assemble and decorate them.

3 Following the instructions on pages 18–19, warm up a pan or plate—you will use this for sticking the half-shells together.

4 To fill your cocoa bombs, spoon 1 tablespoon of caramel flavor hot cocoa mix/drinking chocolate powder into a half-shell, then add 3 caramel candy pieces and 5–7 mini marshmallows, depending on space. Take care not to overfill the shells, as this will make sealing them difficult.

5 Take another empty half-shell and place it carefully, rim-down onto the warm pan or plate. Let the chocolate rim melt for 3–5 seconds, then gently press together with the filled half-shell to seal, following the detailed instructions on pages 18–19. Wipe off any excess chocolate around the rim and set aside in the prepared cupcake liner/case or on the upside-down silicone mold.

6 Repeat with the remaining half-shells and filling to make 3 cocoa bombs.

7 To decorate, drizzle over the remaining tempered dark chocolate following the instructions on page 22. Add a few caramel candy pieces and a pinch of coarse sea salt. Leave for 15–20 minutes at room temperature to allow the decoration to dry.

8 Package the bombs as gifts, or to serve, place a cocoa bomb inside a cup or mug, pour over the hot milk of your choice and watch the bomb explode. Stir to mix evenly and serve warm.

English Toffee Cocoa Bombs

Buttery and warm, English toffee is a candy store favorite for many. The rich flavors of this confection are captured in these mouthwatering cocoa bombs, the sweetness of the toffee pairing beautifully with the slightly bitter dark chocolate.

⅛ teaspoon English toffee extract oil

12 oz./340 g tempered dark chocolate (see pages 14–15)

TO FILL

3 tablespoons English toffee flavor hot cocoa mix/drinking chocolate powder

15–21 mini marshmallows

TO DECORATE

crushed almonds

crushed English toffee pieces

TO SERVE

hot milk of your choice, (allow about 1 cup/ 235 ml per serving)

MAKES 3 COCOA BOMBS

1 Add the English toffee extract oil to the melted tempered chocolate and mix well.

2 Use 10 oz./285 g of the tempered dark chocolate to make 6 cocoa bomb half-shells, following the instructions on pages 16–17, then remove from the molds.

3 Prepare 3 small cupcake liners/cases on a parchment-lined baking sheet, or use a clean silicone mold turned upside down. This will hold the bombs in place as you assemble and decorate them.

4 Following the instructions on pages 18–19, warm up a pan or plate—you will use this for sticking the half-shells together.

5 To fill your cocoa bombs, spoon 1 tablespoon of English toffee flavor hot cocoa mix/drinking chocolate powder into a half-shell, then add 5–7 mini marshmallows, depending on space. Take care not to overfill the shells, as this will make sealing them difficult.

6 Take another empty half-shell and place it carefully, rim-down onto the warm pan or plate. Let the chocolate rim melt for 3–5 seconds, then gently press together with the filled half-shell to seal, following the detailed instructions on page 18–19. Wipe off any excess chocolate around the rim and set aside in the prepared cupcake liner/case or on the upside-down silicone mold.

7 Repeat with the remaining half-shells and filling to make 3 cocoa bombs.

8 To decorate, drizzle over the remaining tempered dark chocolate following the instructions on page 22, then sprinkle each one with some crushed almonds and crushed English toffee pieces. Leave for 15–20 minutes at room temperature to dry.

9 Package the bombs as gifts, or to serve, place a cocoa bomb inside a cup or mug, pour over the hot milk of your choice and watch the bomb explode. Stir to mix evenly and serve warm.

Orange Zest Cocoa Bombs

Orange you glad it's time for more appetizing cocoa bombs?! These give your drink a subtle hint of orange flavor, which perfectly complements the rich taste of dark chocolate. Add a tablespoon of pulp-free orange juice to the final drink if you want the orange taken up a notch.

⅛ teaspoon orange zest extract oil

12 oz./340 g tempered dark chocolate (see pages 14–15)

TO FILL

3 tablespoons dark chocolate hot cocoa mix/drinking chocolate powder

15–21 orange mini marshmallows

TO DECORATE

fresh orange rind pieces or orange slice candy pieces

TO SERVE

hot milk of your choice, (allow about 1 cup/ 235 ml per serving)

MAKES 3 COCOA BOMBS

1 Add the orange zest extract oil to the melted tempered chocolate and mix well.

2 Use 10 oz./285 g of the tempered dark chocolate to make 6 cocoa bomb half-shells, following the instructions on pages 16–17, then remove from the molds.

3 Prepare 3 small cupcake liners/cases on a parchment-lined baking sheet, or use a clean silicone mold turned upside down. This will hold the bombs in place as you assemble and decorate them.

4 Following the instructions on pages 18–19, warm up a pan or plate—you will use this for sticking the half-shells together.

5 To fill your cocoa bombs, spoon 1 tablespoon of dark chocolate hot cocoa mix/drinking chocolate powder into a half-shell, then add 5–7 orange mini marshmallows, depending on space. Take care not to overfill the shells, as this will make sealing them difficult.

6 Take another empty half-shell and place it carefully, rim-down onto the warm pan or plate. Let the chocolate rim melt for 3–5 seconds, then gently press together with the filled half-shell to seal, following the detailed instructions on pages 18–19. Wipe off any excess chocolate around the rim and set aside in the prepared cupcake liner/case or on the upside-down silicone mold.

7 Repeat with the remaining half-shells and filling to make 3 cocoa bombs.

8 To decorate, drizzle over the remaining tempered dark chocolate following the instructions on page 22, then add some fresh orange rind pieces or orange slice candy pieces. Leave for 15–20 minutes at room temperature to dry.

9 Package the bombs as gifts, or to serve, place a cocoa bomb inside a cup or mug, pour over the hot milk of your choice and watch the bomb explode. Stir to mix evenly and serve warm.

Candy Corn Cocoa Bombs

These vibrant cocoa bombs will match all of your fall/autumn aesthetic with gorgeous orange and red hues. This recipe gives your hot cocoa drink a fun orange color, too.

10 oz./285 g tempered white chocolate (see pages 14–15)

TO FILL

3 tablespoons white chocolate hot cocoa mix/drinking chocolate powder

15–21 orange mini marshmallows

TO DECORATE

2 oz./55 g melted red candy melts, for drizzling

2 oz./55 g melted orange candy melts, for drizzling

crushed or whole candy corn pieces

TO SERVE

hot milk of your choice (allow about 1 cup/ 235 ml per serving)

MAKES 3 COCOA BOMBS

1 Use the tempered white chocolate to make 6 cocoa bomb half-shells, following the instructions on pages 16–17, then remove from the molds.

2 Prepare 3 small cupcake liners/cases on a parchment-lined baking sheet, or use a clean silicone mold turned upside down. This will hold the bombs in place as you assemble and decorate them.

3 Following the instructions on pages 18–19, warm up a pan or plate—you will use this for sticking the half-shells together.

4 To fill your cocoa bombs, spoon 1 tablespoon of white chocolate hot cocoa mix/drinking chocolate powder into a half-shell, then add 5–7 orange mini marshmallows, depending on space. Take care not to overfill the shells, as this will make sealing them difficult.

5 Take another empty half-shell and place it carefully, rim-down onto the warm pan or plate. Let the chocolate rim melt for 3–5 seconds, then gently press together with the filled half-shell to seal, following the detailed instructions on pages 18–19. Wipe off any excess chocolate around the rim and set aside in the prepared cupcake liner/case or on the upside-down silicone mold.

6 Repeat with the remaining half-shells and filling to make 3 cocoa bombs.

7 To decorate, drizzle melted red candy melts over each cocoa bomb, followed by orange candy melts in the opposite direction. Finish with crushed or whole candy corn pieces. Leave for 15–20 minutes at room temperature to dry.

8 Package the bombs as gifts, or to serve, place a cocoa bomb inside a cup or mug, pour over the hot milk of your choice and watch the bomb explode. Stir to mix evenly and serve warm.

CHAPTER **5**

Fun Time

Gender Reveal Cocoa Bombs

These gender reveal cocoa bombs are a tasty and stylish way of entertaining baby shower guests. Give them as party favors, serve as refreshments, or use them as a fun way to deliver the grand reveal.

10 oz./285 g tempered white chocolate (see pages 14–15)

TO FILL

3 tablespoons white chocolate hot cocoa mix/drinking chocolate powder

15–21 pink or blue mini marshmallows

TO DECORATE

2 oz./55 g melted pink and/or blue candy melts, for drizzling (see page 22)

pink and/or blue star, pearl, and nonpareil sprinkles

TO SERVE

hot milk of your choice (allow about 1 cup/ 235 ml per serving)

MAKES 3 COCOA BOMBS

1 Use the tempered white chocolate to make 6 cocoa bomb half-shells, following the instructions on pages 16–17, then remove from the molds.

2 Prepare 3 small cupcake liners/cases on a parchment-lined baking sheet, or use a clean silicone mold turned upside down. This will hold the bombs in place as you assemble and decorate them.

3 Following the instructions on pages 18–19, warm up a pan or plate—you will use this for sticking the half-shells together.

4 To fill your cocoa bombs, spoon 1 tablespoon of white chocolate hot cocoa mix/drinking chocolate powder into a half-shell, then add 5–7 pink or blue mini marshmallows, depending on space. Take care not to overfill the shells, as this will make sealing them difficult.

5 Take another empty half-shell and place it carefully, rim-down onto the warm pan or plate. Let the chocolate rim melt for 3–5 seconds, then gently press together with the filled half-shell to seal, following the detailed instructions on pages 18–19. Wipe off any excess chocolate around the rim and set aside in the prepared cupcake liner/case or on the upside-down silicone mold.

6 Repeat with the remaining half-shells and filling to make 3 cocoa bombs.

7 To decorate, drizzle melted pink and/or blue candy melts over each cocoa bomb following the instructions on page 22, then sprinkle each one with some pink and/or blue star, pearl, and nonpareil sprinkles. Leave for 15–20 minutes at room temperature to allow the decoration to dry.

8 Package the bombs as gifts, or to serve, place a cocoa bomb inside a cup or mug, pour over the hot milk of your choice and watch the bomb explode. Stir to mix evenly and serve warm.

Dinosaur Cocoa Bombs

A sure-fire way of keeping your kids entertained for a hot minute, these fun animal treats are perfect to make together on family game nights, movie nights, or even to give on Christmas morning.

10 oz./285 g tempered white chocolate (see pages 14–15)

TO FILL

3 tablespoons milk chocolate hot cocoa mix/drinking chocolate powder

15–21 white mini marshmallows

TO DECORATE

melted white chocolate, for sticking

6 candy eyes

9 candy corn pieces

multicolored sprinkles

TO SERVE

hot milk of your choice (allow about 1 cup/ 235 ml per serving)

MAKES 3 COCOA BOMBS

1 Use the tempered white chocolate to make 6 cocoa bomb half-shells, following the instructions on pages 16–17, then remove from the molds.

2 Prepare 3 small cupcake liners/cases on a parchment-lined baking sheet, or use a clean silicone mold turned upside down. This will hold the bombs in place as you assemble and decorate them.

3 Following the instructions on pages 18–19, warm up a pan or plate—you will use this for sticking the half-shells together.

4 To fill your cocoa bombs, spoon 1 tablespoon of milk chocolate hot cocoa mix/drinking chocolate powder into a half-shell, then add 5–7 mini marshmallows, depending on space. Take care not to overfill the shells, as this will make sealing them difficult.

5 Take another empty half-shell and place it carefully, rim-down onto the warm pan or plate. Let the chocolate rim melt for 3–5 seconds, then gently press together with the filled half-shell to seal, following the detailed instructions on pages 18–19. Wipe off any excess chocolate around the rim and set aside in the prepared cupcake liner/case or on the upside-down silicone mold.

6 Repeat with the remaining half-shells and filling to make 3 cocoa bombs.

7 To decorate, dab a small amount of melted white chocolate onto the back of 2 candy eyes and stick onto each bomb. Dab a generous amount of melted chocolate onto the bottom of 3 candy corn pieces and stick them in a row above the eyes to give the dinosaur its spikes – hold each candy piece in place for 30 seconds or until set. Cover where the chocolate has squashed out around the base of the candy corn with multicolored sprinkles. Leave for 15–20 minutes at room temperature to dry.

8 Package the bombs as gifts, or to serve, place a cocoa bomb inside a cup or mug, pour over the hot milk of your choice and watch the bomb explode. Stir to mix evenly and serve warm.

Birthday Cocoa Bombs

Ring in another year of living on planet earth and treat yourself, your friends, or your loved ones to these unique treats. Enjoy with hot milk alongside the birthday cake or even use these pretty bombs to top the birthday cake itself as decoration.

12 oz./340 g tempered white chocolate (see pages 14–15)

TO FILL
3 tablespoons white chocolate hot cocoa mix/ drinking chocolate powder

3 pinches of mixed rainbow sprinkles

15–21 rainbow or pink mini marshmallows

TO DECORATE
mixed rainbow sprinkles

TO SERVE
hot milk of your choice (allow about 1 cup/ 235 ml per serving)

MAKES 3 COCOA BOMBS

1 Use 10 oz./285 g of the tempered chocolate to make 6 cocoa bomb half-shells, following the instructions on pages 16–17. Remove from the molds. Reserve the remaining chocolate for drizzling.

2 Prepare 3 small cupcake liners/cases on a parchment-lined baking sheet, or use a clean silicone mold turned upside down. This will hold the bombs in place as you assemble and decorate them.

3 Following the instructions on pages 18–19, warm up a pan or plate—you will use this for sticking the half-shells together.

4 To fill your cocoa bombs, spoon 1 tablespoon of white chocolate hot cocoa mix/drinking chocolate powder into a half-shell, then add a pinch of rainbow sprinkles and 5–7 mini marshmallows, depending on space. Take care not to overfill the shells, as this will make sealing them difficult.

5 Take another empty half-shell and place it carefully, rim-down onto the warm pan or plate. Let the chocolate rim melt for 3–5 seconds, then gently press together with the filled half-shell to seal, following the detailed instructions on pages 18–19. Wipe off any excess chocolate around the rim and set aside in the prepared cupcake liner/case or on the upside-down silicone mold.

6 Repeat with the remaining half-shells and filling to make 3 cocoa bombs.

7 To decorate, drizzle over the remaining tempered white chocolate following the instructions on page 22, then sprinkle each one with plenty of rainbow sprinkles. Leave for 15–20 minutes at room temperature to allow the decoration to dry.

8 Package the bombs as gifts, or to serve, place a cocoa bomb inside a cup or mug, pour over the hot milk of your choice and watch the bomb explode. Stir to mix evenly and serve warm.

Unicorn Cocoa Bombs

These magical white chocolate cocoa bombs will delight children and adults alike. Get kids involved with the decorating process, whether you use a unicorn cupcake kit or go with shiny luster dust and sprinkles.

12 oz./340 g tempered white chocolate (see pages 14–15)

TO FILL

3 tablespoons white chocolate hot cocoa mix/drinking chocolate powder

3 tablespoons unicorn mix sprinkles

15–21 pink mini marshmallows

TO DECORATE

1 unicorn cupcake decorating kit (available online)

pink luster dust

unicorn mix sprinkles

TO SERVE

hot milk of your choice (allow about 1 cup/ 235 ml per serving)

MAKES 3 COCOA BOMBS

1 Use 10 oz./285 g of the tempered chocolate to make 6 cocoa bomb half-shells, following the instructions on pages 16–17. Remove from the molds. Reserve the remaining chocolate for drizzling or sticking.

2 Prepare 3 small cupcake liners/cases on a parchment-lined baking sheet, or use a clean silicone mold turned upside down. This will hold the bombs in place as you assemble and decorate them.

3 Following the instructions on pages 18–19, warm up a pan or plate—you will use this for sticking the half-shells together.

4 To fill your cocoa bombs, spoon 1 tablespoon of white chocolate hot cocoa mix/drinking chocolate powder and 1 tablespoon of unicorn mix sprinkles into a half-shell. Add 5–7 mini marshmallows, depending on space. Take care not to overfill the shells, as this will make sealing them difficult.

5 Take another empty half-shell and place it carefully, rim-down onto the warm pan or plate. Let the chocolate rim melt for 3–5 seconds, then gently press together with the filled half-shell to seal, following the detailed instructions on pages 18–19. Wipe off any excess chocolate around the rim and set aside in the prepared cupcake liner/case or on the upside-down silicone mold.

6 Repeat with the remaining half-shells and filling to make 3 cocoa bombs.

7 To decorate the bombs with the cupcake kit, use the remaining tempered white chocolate to stick on the candy ears, eyes, and horn with some sprinkles around the horn. Paint pink luster dust under the eyes to give the unicorn a blushing effect. Alternatively, simply paint the bombs all over with pink luster dust, drizzle with the remaining tempered white chocolate following the instructions on page 22, and top with unicorn mix sprinkles.

8 Package the bombs as gifts, or to serve, place a cocoa bomb inside a cup or mug, pour over the hot milk of your choice and watch the bomb explode. Stir to mix evenly and serve warm.

Reindeer Cocoa Bombs

Transform these simple spheres and bring them to life as cheeky reindeer by using candy eyes, chocolate drops, and pretzels. These adorable cocoa bombs are ALMOST too cute to drink... almost.

10 oz./285 g tempered dark chocolate (see pages 14–15)

TO FILL

3 tablespoons dark chocolate hot cocoa mix/drinking chocolate powder

15–21 white mini marshmallows

TO DECORATE

melted dark chocolate, for sticking

6 candy eyes

6 small pretzel twists

3 red chocolate drops

TO SERVE

hot milk of your choice (allow about 1 cup/ 235 ml per serving)

MAKES 3 COCOA BOMBS

1 Use the tempered dark chocolate to make 6 cocoa bomb half-shells, following the instructions on pages 16–17, then remove from the molds.

2 Prepare 3 small cupcake liners/cases on a parchment-lined baking sheet, or use a clean silicone mold turned upside down. This will hold the bombs in place as you assemble and decorate them.

3 Following the instructions on pages 18–19, warm up a pan or plate—you will use this for sticking the half-shells together.

4 To fill your cocoa bombs, spoon 1 tablespoon of dark chocolate hot cocoa mix/drinking chocolate powder into a half-shell, then add 5–7 mini marshmallows, depending on space. Take care not to overfill the shells, as this will make sealing them difficult.

5 Take another empty half-shell and place it carefully, rim-down onto the warm pan or plate. Let the chocolate rim melt for 3–5 seconds, then gently press together with the filled half-shell to seal, following the detailed instructions on pages 18–19. Wipe off any excess chocolate around the rim and set aside in the prepared cupcake liner/case or on the upside-down silicone mold.

6 Repeat with the remaining half-shells and filling to make 3 cocoa bombs.

7 To decorate, dab the back of the candy eyes with melted chocolate and stick 2 onto each bomb. Carefully cut the bottom of the heart shape off the small pretzel twists and stick 2 of these on as antlers just above the eyes – you may need to hold them in place for around 30 seconds. Finally, bring the reindeer to life by sticking the red chocolate drops on as noses using a little more melted chocolate. Leave for 15–20 minutes at room temperature to dry.

8 Package the bombs as gifts, or to serve, place a cocoa bomb inside a cup or mug, pour over the hot milk of your choice and watch the bomb explode. Stir to mix evenly and serve warm.

Gold Rubber Ducky Cocoa Bombs

These striking golden duck cocoa bombs are the cutest creative twist on classic cocoa bombs. Use them as a way to celebrate spring, Easter, or for young children's birthday parties. Of course, any other animal shaped mold would work in the same way, as long as you temper enough chocolate for the size—let your imagination run wild!

12 oz./340 g tempered caramelized white chocolate (see pages 14–15)

TO FILL

1½ tablespoons milk chocolate hot cocoa mix/drinking chocolate powder

6–9 mini marshmallows

TO DECORATE
gold luster dust

TO SERVE

hot milk of your choice (allow about 1 cup/ 235 ml per serving)

MAKES 3 COCOA BOMBS

1 Paint the cavities of a duck-shaped silicone mold generously with gold luster dust to decorate. Use the tempered chocolate to make 6 cocoa bomb half-shells in the mold, then remove them following the instructions on pages 16–17.

2 Prepare 3 small cupcake liners/cases on a parchment-lined baking sheet, or use a clean silicone mold turned upside down. This will hold the bombs in place as you assemble and decorate them.

3 Following the instructions on pages 18–19, warm up a pan or plate—you will use this for sticking the half-shells together.

4 To fill your cocoa bombs, spoon ½ tablespoon of milk chocolate hot cocoa mix/drinking chocolate powder into a half-shell, then add 2–3 mini marshmallows, depending on space. Take care not to overfill the shells, as this will make sealing them difficult.

5 Take another empty half-shell and place it carefully, rim-down onto the warm pan or plate. Let the chocolate rim melt for 3–5 seconds, then gently press together with the filled half-shell to seal, following the detailed instructions on pages 18–19. Wipe off any excess chocolate around the rim and set aside in the prepared cupcake liner/case or on the upside-down silicone mold.

6 Repeat with the remaining half-shells and filling to make 3 cocoa bombs. Leave for 15–20 minutes at room temperature to set.

7 Package the bombs as gifts, or to serve, place a cocoa bomb inside a cup or mug, pour over the hot milk of your choice and watch the bomb explode. Stir to mix evenly and serve warm.

CHAPTER 6

Seasonal Sensations

Luck of the Irish Cocoa Bombs

These colorful cocoa bombs are an excellent way to celebrate St. Patrick's Day. The best part about these beauties is that they pair magnificently with a shot of Irish whiskey cream.

10 oz./285 g tempered dark chocolate (see pages 14–15)

TO FILL

3 pinches of gold sugar crystals

15–21 green mini marshmallows

TO DECORATE

2 oz./55 g melted green candy melts, for drizzling

shamrock-shaped sprinkles/St. Patrick's Day-themed sprinkles

TO SERVE

hot milk of your choice (allow about 1 cup/ 235 ml per serving)

3 shots (3 fl. oz./90 ml) Irish whiskey cream

MAKES 3 COCOA BOMBS

1 Use the tempered dark chocolate to make 6 cocoa bomb half-shells, following the instructions on pages 16–17, then remove from the molds.

2 Prepare 3 small cupcake liners/cases on a parchment-lined baking sheet, or use a clean silicone mold turned upside down. This will hold the bombs in place as you assemble and decorate them.

3 Following the instructions on pages 18–19, warm up a pan or plate—you will use this for sticking the half-shells together.

4 To fill your cocoa bombs, add a pinch of gold sugar crystals and 5–7 green mini marshmallows to a half-shell. Take care not to overfill the shells, as this will make sealing them difficult.

5 Take another empty half-shell and place it carefully, rim-down onto the warm pan or plate. Let the chocolate rim melt for 3–5 seconds, then gently press together with the filled half-shell to seal, following the detailed instructions on pages 18–19. Wipe off any excess chocolate around the rim and set aside in the prepared cupcake liner/case or on the upside-down silicone mold.

6 Repeat with the remaining half-shells and filling to make 3 cocoa bombs.

7 To decorate, drizzle melted green candy melts over each cocoa bomb following the instructions on page 22, then sprinkle each one with some shamrock-shaped sprinkles/St. Patrick's Day-themed sprinkles. Leave for 15–20 minutes at room temperature to allow the decoration to dry.

8 Package the bombs as gifts, or to serve, place a cocoa bomb inside a cup or mug, pour over the hot milk of your choice and watch the bomb explode. Finish with 1 shot (1 fl. oz./30 ml) of Irish whiskey cream. Stir to mix evenly and serve warm.

Strawberry White Chocolate Cocoa Bombs

Melt your significant other's heart with these heart-shaped strawberry and white chocolate cocoa bombs. Perfect for Valentine's day, special anniversaries, or a Tuesday afternoon just because they are delicious.

12 oz./340 g tempered white chocolate (see pages 14–15)

TO FILL

3 teaspoons white chocolate hot cocoa mix/drinking chocolate powder

3 teaspoons freeze-dried strawberry powder

9–12 pink mini heart-shaped marshmallows or white mini marshmallows

TO DECORATE

freeze-dried strawberry pieces or heart-shaped sprinkles

TO SERVE

hot strawberry milk or milk of your choice (allow about 1 cup/ 235 ml per serving)

MAKES 3 COCOA BOMBS

1 Use 10 oz./285 g of the tempered chocolate to make 6 cocoa bomb half-shells in heart-shaped molds, following the instructions on pages 16–17. Remove from the molds. Reserve the remaining chocolate for drizzling.

2 Prepare 3 small cupcake liners/cases on a parchment-lined baking sheet, or use a clean silicone mold turned upside down. This will hold the bombs in place as you assemble and decorate them.

3 Following the instructions on pages 18–19, warm up a pan or plate—you will use this for sticking the half-shells together.

4 To fill your cocoa bombs, spoon 1 teaspoon of white chocolate hot cocoa mix/drinking chocolate powder into a half-shell, then add 1 teaspoon of freeze-dried strawberry powder, and 3–4 mini marshmallows depending on space. Take care not to overfill the shells, as this will make sealing them difficult.

5 Take another empty half-shell and place it carefully, rim-down onto the warm pan or plate. Let the chocolate rim melt for 3–5 seconds, then gently press together with the filled half-shell to seal, following the detailed instructions on pages 18–19. Wipe off any excess chocolate around the rim and set aside in the prepared cupcake liner/case or on the upside-down silicone mold.

6 Repeat with the remaining half-shells and filling to make 3 cocoa bombs.

7 To decorate, drizzle over the remaining tempered white chocolate following the instructions on page 22, then sprinkle each one with some freeze-dried strawberry pieces or heart-shaped sprinkles. Leave for 15–20 minutes at room temperature to dry.

8 Package the bombs as gifts, or to serve, place a cocoa bomb inside a cup or mug, pour over the hot strawberry milk or milk of your choice and watch the bomb explode. Stir to mix evenly and serve warm.

Easter Egg Cocoa Bombs

What better time to gift this egg-ceptional version of a cocoa bomb than Easter? In this recipe, we fill these cute little chocolate eggs with mini pastel-colored marshmallows for a stunning melting moment.

12 oz./340 g tempered milk chocolate (see pages 14–15)

TO FILL

3 tablespoons milk chocolate hot cocoa mix/drinking chocolate powder

15–21 mini pastel-colored marshmallows

TO DECORATE

mixed pastel-colored sprinkles

TO SERVE

hot milk of your choice (allow about 1 cup/ 235 ml per serving)

MAKES 3 COCOA BOMBS

1 Use 10 oz./285 g of the tempered chocolate to make 6 cocoa bomb half-shells, in egg-shaped silicone molds, following the instructions on pages 16–17, then remove from the molds. Reserve the remaining chocolate for drizzling.

2 Prepare 3 small cupcake liners/cases on a parchment-lined baking sheet, or use a clean silicone mold turned upside down. This will hold the bombs in place as you assemble and decorate them.

3 Following the instructions on pages 18–19, warm up a pan or plate—you will use this for sticking the half-shells together.

4 To fill your cocoa bombs, spoon 1 tablespoon of milk chocolate hot cocoa mix/drinking chocolate powder into a half-shell, then add 5–7 mini pastel-colored marshmallows, depending on space. Take care not to overfill the shells, as this will make sealing them difficult.

5 Take another empty half-shell and place it carefully, rim-down onto the warm pan or plate. Let the chocolate rim melt for 3–5 seconds, then gently press together with the filled half-shell to seal, following the detailed instructions on pages 18–19. Wipe off any excess chocolate around the rim and set aside in the prepared cupcake liner/case or on the upside-down silicone mold.

6 Repeat with the remaining half-shells and filling to make 3 cocoa bombs.

7 To decorate, drizzle over the remaining tempered milk chocolate following the instructions on page 22, then sprinkle each one with plenty of pastel-colored sprinkles. Leave for 15–20 minutes at room temperature to allow the decoration to dry.

8 Package the bombs as gifts, or to serve, place a cocoa bomb inside a cup or mug, pour over the hot milk of your choice and watch the bomb explode. Stir to mix evenly and serve warm.

Golden Caramel White Chocolate Cocoa Bombs

These golden orbs of goodness are as delicious as they are pretty. Add some festive spooky sprinkles for fall/autumn or Halloween-themed parties, or prepare as a fun trick-or-treat gift.

12 oz./340 g tempered caramelized white chocolate (see pages 14–15)

TO FILL

3 tablespoons caramel flavor hot cocoa mix/drinking chocolate powder

15–21 white mini marshmallows

TO DECORATE

gold luster dust (see page 22)

Halloween sprinkles

TO SERVE

hot milk of your choice (allow about 1 cup/235 ml per serving)

MAKES 3 COCOA BOMBS

1 Use 10 oz./285 g of the tempered chocolate to make 6 cocoa bomb half-shells, following the instructions on pages 16–17. Remove from the molds. Reserve the remaining chocolate for drizzling.

2 Prepare 3 small cupcake liners/cases on a parchment-lined baking sheet, or use a clean silicone mold turned upside down. This will hold the bombs in place as you assemble and decorate them.

3 Following the instructions on pages 18–19, warm up a pan or plate—you will use this for sticking the half-shells together.

4 To fill your cocoa bombs, spoon 1 tablespoon of caramel flavor hot cocoa mix/drinking chocolate powder into a half-shell, then add 5–7 mini marshmallows, depending on space. Take care not to overfill the shells, as this will make sealing them difficult.

5 Take another empty half-shell and place it carefully, rim-down onto the warm pan or plate. Let the chocolate rim melt for 3–5 seconds, then gently press together with the filled half-shell to seal, following the detailed instructions on pages 18–19. Wipe off any excess chocolate around the rim and set aside in the prepared cupcake liner/case or on the upside-down silicone mold.

6 Repeat with the remaining half-shells and filling to make 3 cocoa bombs.

7 To decorate, paint streaks of gold luster dust over the top of each bomb. Drizzle over the remaining tempered caramelized white chocolate following the instructions on page 22, then sprinkle with some Halloween sprinkles. Leave for 15–20 minutes at room temperature to dry.

8 Package the bombs as gifts, or to serve, place a cocoa bomb inside a cup or mug, pour over the hot milk of your choice and watch the bomb explode. Stir to mix evenly and serve warm.

Crushed Peppermint Cocoa Bombs

To me, nothing screams winter like peppermint flavor candy and nothing screams Christmas like these crushed peppermint cocoa bombs. The red and white candy with the green marshmallows is the perfect festive color palette.

12 oz./340 g tempered dark chocolate (see pages 14–15)

TO FILL

3 tablespoons dark chocolate hot cocoa mix/drinking chocolate powder

3 teaspoons crushed peppermint candy pieces

15–21 mini peppermint flavor marshmallows

TO DECORATE

crushed peppermint candy pieces

TO SERVE

3 candy canes (optional)

hot milk of your choice (allow about 1 cup/235 ml per serving)

MAKES 3 COCOA BOMBS

1. Use 10 oz./285 g of the tempered chocolate to make 6 cocoa bomb half-shells, following the instructions on pages 16–17. Remove from the molds. Reserve the remaining chocolate for drizzling..

2. Prepare 3 small cupcake liners/cases on a parchment-lined baking sheet, or use a clean silicone mold turned upside down. This will hold the bombs in place as you assemble and decorate them.

3. Following the instructions on pages 18–19, warm up a pan or plate—you will use this for sticking the half-shells together.

4. To fill your cocoa bombs, spoon 1 tablespoon of dark chocolate hot cocoa mix/drinking chocolate powder into a half-shell, then add 1 teaspoon of crushed peppermint candy pieces and 5–7 mini peppermint flavor marshmallows, depending on space. Take care not to overfill the shells, as this will make sealing them difficult.

5. Take another empty half-shell and place it carefully, rim-down onto the warm pan or plate. Let the chocolate rim melt for 3–5 seconds, then gently press together with the filled half-shell to seal, following the detailed instructions on pages 18–19. Wipe off any excess chocolate around the rim and set aside in the prepared cupcake liner/case or on the upside-down silicone mold.

6. Repeat with the remaining half-shells and filling to make 3 cocoa bombs.

7. To decorate, drizzle over the remaining tempered dark chocolate following the instructions on page 22, then sprinkle each one with some crushed peppermint candy pieces. Leave for 15–20 minutes at room temperature to allow the decoration to dry.

8. Package the bombs as gifts, or to serve, place a cocoa bomb inside a cup or mug and add a candy cane, if you like. Pour over the hot milk of your choice and watch the bomb explode. Stir to mix evenly and serve warm.

Snowman Cocoa Bombs

Anyone would be delighted to receive one of these adorable snowman cocoa bombs over the festive period. They have so much personality you almost feel bad for drowning them in hot milk.

10 oz./285 g tempered white chocolate (see pages 14–15)

TO FILL

3 tablespoons white chocolate hot cocoa mix/drinking chocolate powder

15–21 white mini marshmallows

TO DECORATE

6 candy eyes

3 large white marshmallows

3 orange chocolate drops

melted dark chocolate, for piping and sticking (see page 22)

3 small pretzels

TO SERVE

hot milk of your choice (allow about 1 cup/235 ml per serving)

MAKES 3 COCOA BOMBS

1 Use the tempered white chocolate to make 6 cocoa bomb half-shells, following the instructions on pages 16–17, then remove from the molds.

2 Prepare 3 small cupcake liners/cases on a parchment-lined baking sheet, or use a clean silicone mold turned upside down. This will hold the bombs in place as you assemble and decorate them.

3 Following the instructions on pages 18–19, warm up a pan or plate—you will use this for sticking the half-shells together.

4 To fill your cocoa bombs, spoon 1 tablespoon of white chocolate hot cocoa mix/drinking chocolate powder into a half-shell, then add 5–7 mini marshmallows. Take care not to overfill the shells.

5 Take another empty half-shell and place it carefully, rim-down onto the warm pan or plate. Let the chocolate rim melt for 3–5 seconds, then gently press together with the filled half-shell to seal, following the detailed instructions on pages 18–19. Wipe off any excess chocolate around the rim and set aside in the prepared cupcake liner/case or on the upside-down silicone mold.

6 Repeat with the remaining half-shells and filling to make 3 cocoa bombs.

7 To decorate, stick the candy eyes onto the large marshmallows using the melted chocolate, then add orange chocolate drops as noses. Paint or pipe a smile in melted chocolate onto each of the large marshmallows, then paint or pipe 3 buttons onto the cocoa bombs. Cut the small pretzels in half and stick each half into the underside of the marshmallows as snowmen arms.

8 Gently stick the marshmallow heads to the cocoa bombs with a little melted chocolate, being careful to align the faces and arms with the buttons, and holding for 30 seconds or until set. Leave for 15–20 minutes at room temperature to allow the decoration to dry.

9 Package the bombs as gifts, or to serve, place a cocoa bomb inside a cup or mug, pour over the hot milk of your choice and watch the bomb explode. Stir to mix evenly and serve warm.

Christmas Lights Cocoa Bomb

These chocolate ornaments will light up your holiday cookie platter, should you choose to display them there. Friends and family will be enchanted by this festive cocoa bomb creation.

10 oz./285 g tempered dark chocolate (see pages 14–15)

TO FILL

3 tablespoons milk chocolate hot cocoa mix/drinking chocolate powder

3 large Christmas tree-shaped marshmallows or 15–21 mini white marshmallows

TO DECORATE

2 oz./55 g tempered white chocolate, for drizzling

green, red, and white chocolate drops or pearls

TO SERVE

hot milk of your choice (allow about 1 cup/ 235 ml per serving)

MAKES 3 COCOA BOMBS

1 Use the tempered dark chocolate to make 6 cocoa bomb half-shells, following the instructions on pages 16–17, then remove from the molds.

2 Prepare 3 small cupcake liners/cases on a parchment-lined baking sheet, or use a clean silicone mold turned upside down. This will hold the bombs in place as you assemble and decorate them.

3 Following the instructions on pages 14–17, warm up a pan or plate—you will use this for sticking the half-shells together.

4 To fill your cocoa bombs, spoon 1 tablespoon of milk chocolate hot cocoa mix/drinking chocolate powder into a half-shell, then add 1 large Christmas tree-shaped marshmallow or 5–7 mini marshmallows, depending on space. Take care not to overfill the shells, as this will make sealing them difficult.

5 Take another empty half-shell and place it carefully, rim-down onto the warm pan or plate. Let the chocolate rim melt for 3–5 seconds, then gently press together with the filled half-shell to seal, following the detailed instructions on pages 18–19. Wipe off any excess chocolate around the rim and set aside in the prepared cupcake liner/case or on the upside-down silicone mold.

6 Repeat with the remaining half-shells and filling to make 3 cocoa bombs.

7 To decorate, drizzle or pipe 3–4 lines of white chocolate in opposite directions over each cocoa bomb in a cross-hatch pattern following the instructions on pages 18–19. Add green, red, and white chocolate drops or pearls where the lines meet. Leave for 15–20 minutes at room temperature to allow the decoration to dry.

8 Package the bombs as gifts, or to serve, place a cocoa bomb inside a cup or mug, pour over the hot milk of your choice and watch the bomb explode. Stir to mix evenly and serve warm.

The Original Cocoa Bomb

There is no better way to end something than saving the best for last. This simple recipe is what made cocoa bombs all the rage around the world. Using 3 simple ingredients, this global winter icon was innovated in late 2019. This recipe was originally meant to be enjoyed over Christmas. However you decide to enjoy it, just know that we are very grateful for making it this far along.

10 oz./285 g tempered milk chocolate (see pages 14–15)

TO FILL
6–9 mini snowman-shaped marshmallows

TO DECORATE
gold luster dust

TO SERVE
hot milk of your choice (allow about 1 cup/ 235 ml per serving)

MAKES 3 COCOA BOMBS

1 Use the tempered milk chocolate to make 6 cocoa bomb half-shells, following the instructions on pages 16–17, then remove from the molds.

2 Prepare 3 small cupcake liners/cases on a parchment-lined baking sheet, or use a clean silicone mold turned upside down. This will hold the bombs in place as you assemble and decorate them.

3 Following the instructions on pages 18–19, warm up a pan or plate—you will use this for sticking the half-shells together.

4 To fill your cocoa bombs, add 2–3 mini snowman-shaped marshmallows, depending on space. Take care not to overfill the shells, as this will make sealing them difficult.

5 Take another empty half-shell and place it carefully, rim-down onto the warm pan or plate. Let the chocolate rim melt for 3–5 seconds, then gently press together with the filled half-shell to seal, following the detailed instructions on pages 18–19. Wipe off any excess chocolate around the rim and set aside in the prepared cupcake liner/case or on the upside-down silicone mold.

6 Repeat with the remaining half-shells and filling to make 3 cocoa bombs.

7 To decorate, paint gold luster dust all over the cocoa bombs. Leave for 15–20 minutes at room temperature to set.

8 Package the bombs as gifts, or to serve, place a cocoa bomb inside a cup or mug, pour over the hot milk of your choice and watch the bomb explode. Stir to mix evenly and serve warm.

Suppliers

UK Suppliers

Keylink

All things chocolate! Great company and very helpful on the phone with advice if you are starting out.

www.keylink.org

Callebaut

Suppliers of good quality chocolate.

www.callebaut.com

Cacao Barry

Suppliers of good quality chocolate.

www.cacao-barry.com

Home Chocolate Factory

Molds used in this book are available here.

www.homechocolatefactory.com

Vantage House

Molds used in this book are available here.

www.vantagehouse.com

Ask Mummy and Daddy

Lots of fun sweets are available here.

www.askmummyanddaddy.com

Baking Time Club

Suppliers of sprinkles and decorations.

www.etsy.com/shop/BakingTimeClub

Hannah Loves Cake

Suppliers of sprinkles and decorations.

www.etsy.com/shop/HannahLovesCake

Sprinkles and Toppers Ltd

More sprinkles and decorations.

www.etsy.com/shop/sprinklestoppersltd

Nisbets

Suppliers of kitchen equipment.

www.nisbets.co.uk

Also Sainsburys, Waitrose, and Amazon.co.uk

US Suppliers

Amoretti

Suppliers of flavor extract oils.

www.amoretti.com

Callebaut

Suppliers of good quality chocolate.

www.callebaut.com

Concepts in Candy

Supplier of luster dusts and molds.

www.conceptsincandy.com

And Amazon.com

Index

A

almond milk: vegan cocoa bomb 37
almonds: English toffee cocoa
    bombs 87
apple cider: butterscotch apple crisp
    cocoa bombs 72

B

birthday cocoa bombs 98
bourbon whiskey cocoa bombs 56
butterscotch apple crisp cocoa
    bombs 72

C

candy 13, 20
    candy corn cocoa bombs 91
cappuccino tiramisù cocoa bombs
    63
caramel 13
    butterscotch apple crisp cocoa
        bombs 72
    dulce de leche cocoa bombs 68
    golden caramel white chocolate
        cocoa bombs 115
    salted caramel cocoa bombs 84
cayenne: Mexican cinnamon cocoa
    bombs 48
chai tea latte powder: spiced chai
    cocoa bombs 44
chocolate 12
    filling and sealing the half-shells
        18–19
    making half-shells 16–17
    melting and working
        temperatures 15
    tempering chocolate 14–19
    see also dark chocolate; milk
        chocolate; white chocolate
chocolate spread 13
    hazelnut praline cocoa bombs 83
Christmas lights cocoa bomb 120
cider: butterscotch apple crisp cocoa
    bombs 72

cinnamon
    butterscotch apple crisp cocoa
        bombs 72
    horchata 47
    Mexican cinnamon cocoa bombs
        48
cocoa mix, hot 12
cocoa powder
    cappuccino tiramisù cocoa bombs
        63
    vegan cocoa bomb 37
coconut: coconut paradise cocoa
    bomb 80
coconut milk: vegan cocoa bomb 37
coffee 12
    cappuccino tiramisù cocoa bombs
        63
    mocha breve cocoa bombs 51
    white chocolate coffee cocoa
        bombs 41
cookies 20
    cookies and cream cocoa bombs
        64
crackers 20
    s'mores cocoa bombs 79
cream: dulce de leche cocoa bombs
    68
crème brûlée cocoa bombs 60
crushed peppermint cocoa bombs
    116

D

dark chocolate
    bourbon whiskey cocoa bombs 56
    cappuccino tiramisù cocoa bombs
        63
    Christmas lights cocoa bomb 120
    coconut paradise cocoa bomb 80
    crushed peppermint cocoa bombs
        116
    dark chocolate cocoa bomb 29
    English toffee cocoa bombs 87
    the everything cocoa bomb 34
    French vanilla cocoa bombs 52
    hazelnut praline cocoa bombs 83
    high-protein cocoa bomb 38

luck of the Irish cocoa bombs 108
Mexican cinnamon cocoa bombs
    48
mocha breve cocoa bombs 51
orange zest cocoa bombs 88
pumpkin spice cocoa bombs 55
raspberry cocoa bombs 71
reindeer cocoa bombs 102
salted caramel cocoa bombs 84
spiced chai cocoa bombs 44
vegan cocoa bomb 37
decorating techniques 20–3
    ingredients 20–2
    tips for success 23
dinosaur cocoa bombs 97
drinking chocolate powder 12
drizzles 22
dulce de leche cocoa bombs 68

E

Easter egg cocoa bombs 112
English toffee cocoa bombs 87
equipment 10
the everything cocoa bomb 34

F

French vanilla cocoa bombs 52
fudge brownie protein powder:
    high-protein cocoa bomb 38

G

gender reveal cocoa bombs 94
gold rubber ducky cocoa bombs 105
golden caramel white chocolate
    cocoa bombs 115
graham crackers: s'mores cocoa
    bombs 79

H

half-shells
    filling and sealing 18–19
    making 16–17
hazelnut praline cocoa bombs 83
high-protein cocoa bomb 38
horchata 47

I

ingredients 12–13
  decorating 20–2
Irish whiskey cream: luck of the Irish
  cocoa bombs 108

L

luck of the Irish cocoa bombs 108
luster dust 22

M

marshmallows 13
  see also individual recipes
matcha powder: white chocolate and
  matcha cocoa bombs 67
Mexican cinnamon cocoa bombs 48
milk chocolate
  Easter egg cocoa bombs 112
  the everything cocoa bomb 34
  milk chocolate cocoa bomb 30
  the original cocoa bomb 123
  peanut butter cup cocoa bombs
    76
  s'mores cocoa bombs 79
mocha frappe powder
  mocha breve cocoa bombs 51
  white chocolate coffee cocoa
    bombs 41

N

nutmeg: horchata 47

O

oils, extract 13
orange zest cocoa bombs 88
the original cocoa bomb 123

P

packaging ideas 24
peanut butter cup cocoa bombs 76
peppermint cocoa bombs 116
pretzels
  reindeer cocoa bombs 102
  snowman cocoa bombs 119
protein powder: high-protein cocoa
  bomb 38
pumpkin spice cocoa bombs 55

R

raspberry cocoa bombs 71
reindeer cocoa bombs 102
rice milk: horchata 47

S

salted caramel cocoa bombs 84
serving ideas 13, 24
s'mores cocoa bombs 79
snowman cocoa bombs 119
spices 12
  spiced chai cocoa bombs 44
sprinkles 20
strawberry white chocolate cocoa
  bombs 111

T

tea 12
tempering chocolate 14–19
tiramisu cocoa bombs, cappuccino
  63
toffee: English toffee cocoa bombs
  87

U

unicorn cocoa bombs 101

V

vanilla: French vanilla cocoa bombs
  52
vegan cocoa bomb 37

W

whiskey
  bourbon whiskey cocoa bombs 56
  luck of the Irish cocoa bombs 108
white chocolate
  birthday cocoa bombs 98
  candy corn cocoa bombs 91
  cappuccino tiramisù cocoa bombs
    63
  cookies and cream cocoa bombs
    64
  crème brûlée cocoa bombs 60
  dinosaur cocoa bombs 97
  dulce de leche cocoa bombs 68
  the everything cocoa bomb 34

gender reveal cocoa bombs 94
gold rubber ducky cocoa bombs
  105
golden caramel white chocolate
  cocoa bombs 115
horchata 47
snowman cocoa bombs 119
strawberry white chocolate cocoa
  bombs 111
unicorn cocoa bombs 101
white chocolate and matcha cocoa
  bombs 67
white chocolate cocoa bomb 33
white chocolate coffee cocoa
  bombs 41

Acknowledgments

I would like to start by thanking my dear mother, Pilar. *¡Gracias mamá por toda tu dedicación, sacrificios, y apoyo!* I would also like to acknowledge my hard working father, Gerardo. *¡Gracias padre por tu guía y palabras de sabiduría!* Los quiero mucho. I would also like to recognize my siblings, Jerry, Viviana, and Aaron for being a part of this sweet journey. *A mi tía Consuelo, muchas gracias por ser parte de mi vida desde pequeño y por el inmenso apoyo.*

To Father Jose, Bobbie, and the St. Bernard's Catholic Church; thank you for providing me with the space I needed to begin this journey during the first few years of business. God bless! To Joe, Curtis, and Cannon Builders Inc.; I cannot express how eternally grateful I am. More importantly, I appreciate you all for taking a chance on me. I will forever remember this act of kindness with my heart and soul for the rest of my life. A very special acknowledgment to Fernando for driving hours away in the middle of winter to help me during the busiest time of the year. Thank you for being an amazing and supportive partner! Thank you to these individuals and organizations who have been a part of helping me get the company to where it is today: Cody Garrett, Martha Gonzales, David Wagers/Idaho Candy Co., Marie Baker, Susie Rios, Kent Neupert, David Arkoosh, and Boise State University.

Finally, thank you to Cindy Richards, Leslie Harrington, Julia Charles and the rest of the team at RPS for giving me the opportunity to publish this book. A special thank you to Harriet Hudson for her skill in making the bombs for the shoot, Luis Peral for props, and Alex Luck for photographing them so beautifully.